New Horizons for Policy Practice

This book provides fresh perspectives on the state of policy practice. Leading scholars explore such vital conceptual topics as how to impact social justice, what the strengths-based perspective means to policy practitioners and how to bridge the all-too common gap between community organizing and direct practice in social work.

Other esteemed academics address topics including how to use technology to increase social justice, what the impacts of the recent changes in the United States' Supreme Court will be, how to conceptualize the effect of ex-prisoners' re-entry into society and how to better include marginalized populations in the policy practice. The volume closes with two pieces relating to students: using service learning to increase knowledge of macro interventions and integrating social capital analysis into policy practice.

Each topic is thoroughly covered by experts, using the latest scholarly material available. The reader will come away with a new perspective on the many areas where social work is involved, needed and effective in making positive change in the world.

This book was published as a special issue of the *Journal of Policy Practice*.

Richard Hoefer, is Professor at the School of Social Work, University of Texas at Arlington. He specializes in the areas of social policy and program administration, with a particular emphasis on advocacy and program evaluation. Dr. Hoefer is the founding editor of the *Journal of Policy Practice* (formerly the Social Policy Journal). He is the author of *Advocacy Practice for Social Justice*, and numerous articles on topics such as advocacy, non-profit management and program evaluation.

New Horizons for Policy Practice

Edited by Richard Hoefer

 Routledge
Taylor & Francis Group

LONDON AND NEW YORK

First published 2009 by Routledge
2 Park Square, Milton Park, Abingdon, Oxon, OX14 4RN

Simultaneously published in the USA and Canada
by Routledge
711 Third Avenue, New York, NY 10017

Routledge is an imprint of the Taylor & Francis Group, an informa business

© 2009 Edited by Richard Hoefer
First issued in paperback 2013

Typeset in Times by Value Chain, India
Printed and bound in Great Britain by IBT Global

British Library Cataloguing in Publication Data
A catalogue record for this book is available from the British Library

ISBN13: 978-0-415-99815-4 hbk
ISBN13: 978-0-415-84970-8 pbk

CONTENTS

Notes on Contributors   *vii*

1 Introduction   1
   Richard Hoefer

2 The Path to Social Justice Goes Through
   Politics and Economics   4
   David Dempsey

3 A Strengths-Based Framework for Social Policy:
   Barriers and Possibilities   16
   Katharine Hill

4 Bridging the Divide Between Community Organizing Efforts
   and Direct Services in Traditional Social Service Agencies:
   Lessons Learned from a Case Study   32
   Eli Bartle
   Beth Halaas

5 Technology-Based Approaches to Social Work
   and Social Justice   50
   Judith M. Dunlop
   Graham Fawcett

6 The Supreme Court Shuffle: What It Means for Social Work   65
   Sunny Harris Rome
   Carolyn I. Polowy

7 Ex-Prisoners' Re-Entry: An Emerging Frontier
   and a Social Work Challenge   88
   Ram A. Cnaan
   Jeffrey Draine
   Beverly Frazier
   Jill W. Sinha

8   Inclusion in the Policy Process: An Agenda for Participation
    of the Marginalized   109
    Margaret Lombe
    Michael Sherraden

9   Service Learning: The Road from the Classroom
    to Community-Based Macro Intervention   124
    Diane L. Scott

10 Teaching Students to Become Effective in Policy Practice:
    Integrating Social Capital into Social Work
    Education and Practice   136
    Robin L. Ersing
    Diane N. Loeffler

    Index   149

Notes on Contributors

Eli Bartle, MSW, PhD, is Associate Professor, and Beth Halaas, MSW, is Director of Field Education, Social Work Department, California State University at Northridge, Northridge, California.

Ram A. Cnaan, Jeffrey Draine, and Beverly Frazier are affiliated with the School of Social Policy & Practice, University of Pennsylvania.

David Dempsey, ASCW, is the director of DJD Enterprises, a private political social worker consulting firm. He retired in 2005 from his position of Manager, Government Relations and Political Action at the National Association of Social Workers (NASW).

Judith M. Dunlop, MSW, PhD, is Associate Professor, School of Social Work, King's University College at the University of Western Ontario, London, Ontario, Canada.

Robin L. Ersing, PhD, is Assistant Professor at the University of South Florida School of Social Work, Tampa, Florida.

Graham Fawcett is Application Developer and Consultant, Centre for Teaching and Learning, University of Windsor, Windsor, Ontario, Canada.

Katharine M. Hill, MSW, MPP, LISW is a PhD student at the University of Minnesota School of Social Work, St. Paul, Minnesota. She received her MSW from the University of Minnesota School of Social Work and her MPP from the Humphrey Institute of Public Affairs at the University of Minnesota.

Diane N. Loeffler, PhD, is Lecturer in the College of Social Work at the University of Kentucky.

Margaret Lombe, PhD, is Assistant Professor, Graduate School of Social Work, Boston College; Faculty Associate, Center for Social Development, Washington University in St. Louis, Missouri.

Carolyn I. Polowy, JD, is general Counsel, National Association of Social Workers, 750 First Street, N.E., Washington, DC 20002.

Sunny Harris Rome, MSW, JD is Associate Professor of Social Work, George Mason University, Arlington, Virginia.

Diane L. Scott, PhD, is affiliated with the University of West Florida.

Michael Sherraden, PhD, is Benjamin E. Youngdahl Professor of Social Development, and Director of the Center for Social Development, Washington University in St. Louis, Missouri.

Jill W. Sinha is affiliated with the School of Social Work, Rutgers, The State University of New Jersey.

Introduction

This collection of manuscripts has been assembled with the express purpose of showing current thinking about the future of policy practice. You will not find much hardcore research here in terms of quantitative analysis, nor much qualitative research either.

Sometimes it is a very useful, indeed, mandatory, task to stop, look around at the world, and see what might be coming our way. Keen observation, coupled with hard thinking about the looming future, can help us make course corrections and end up closer to our desired outcomes. Such is the case with social policy and policy practice. Political changes are on the horizon with the election of President Obama and more Democrats in the US Congress pushing aside Republican policies of the past eight years. Despite the world wide economic recession, these changes may allow new initiatives to bear fruit in the social policy arena, so it is vital to think deeply about what we want, what our priorities are, and what we would be willing to give up to achieve a good result. I hope you find these papers useful in gaining a broader view of our current and future situations.

The nine articles included in this issue are divided into three groups. The first group consists of conceptual articles relating to social policy and policy practice. We begin with what is in essence an editorial by David Dempsey, former lobbyist for the National Association of Social Workers in Washington, DC. Reflecting on his experiences in the nation's capital and elsewhere, Dempsey argues for a reformulation of social work policy practice theory to include hefty doses of training in political science and economics. Doing so would improve social workers' ability to advocate for and achieve social justice objectives. Although his recommendations are important for social work educators to implement, they are also important for social workers already in the field who desire to improve their policy practice skills.

The second conceptual article is by Katharine Hill. Building on previous work by noted strengths-based scholars, she describes the barriers to and possibilities of actually achieving strengths-based social policy. She also applies her ideas to a specific policy in order to show the usefulness of the framework she has developed. This article continues and advances the discussion in the literature regarding how to define and develop policy that is based on the strengths of a population rather than its problems.

Eli Bartle and Beth Halaas provide a look at how social workers can bridge the current divide between policy practice in a community setting with direct service provision in traditional social service agencies. Using their experiences in a campaign for living wages, they ask important questions such as "Why don't social workers support activist efforts more consistently?" and "What are the barriers to participation of traditional social service agencies in progressive movements?" As we examine how to improve policy practice, answers to such questions help us understand viewpoints of other social workers and learn how to create strategies that can overcome their reluctance to take a stand.

Judith Dunlop and Graham Fawcett author the final conceptual article. They present information regarding the ways that policy practitioners can use technology for electronic advocacy. This article brings us beyond a description of what is "out there" in terms of technology to discuss the "how to use," "why to use," and "how to overcome resistance to using technology in these ways" that sometimes bedevils human service policy practitioners.

The next group of articles is also practice-oriented, but not as conceptual in nature. These three articles point out changing or emerging topics of interest to social policy and social work. Sunny Harris Rome and Carolyn Polowy explore recent changes in the composition and decisions of the United States Supreme Court. As the final arbiters of what is constitutional and what is not, this body of nine people wields tremendous power and authority. Harris and Polowy explain how appointments of conservative justices by former President Bush have changed the decisions of the Court and the likely impacts on social work and our clients. They also urge engagement in efforts to influence the judicial branch, an avenue that policy practitioners frequently overlook.

Ram Cnaan, Jeffrey Draine, Beverly Frazier and Jill Sinha write of an emerging policy concern—what to do with the increasing numbers of men and women emerging from jails and prisons. This population has trouble re-entering society due to difficulties encountered in obtaining housing, employment and education. These barriers, difficult enough to overcome in themselves, are exacerbated by significant mental health and substance addiction problems. The authors suggest ways to cope with these challenges, particularly recommending more comprehensive services at the local level.

Margaret Lombe and Michael Sherraden bring to our attention the exclusion of marginalized groups from the policy process. They argue that social work as a profession needs to pay more attention to including marginalized populations of all types. Lombe and Sherraden call for a "society for all" and show ways to create space at the table for individuals and groups currently excluded.

The final group of articles directs our attention directly to policy practice education. Whereas the previous articles certainly can apply to social work education, these two articles specifically look at issues of educating future policy practitioners. Diane Scott links social work education to the now-popular concept of service learning. She describes how to take a course on community-based macro practice and create a community-based intervention using service learning techniques.

In the final article, Robin Ersing and Diane Loeffler describe how to use the ideas of social capital to teach students how to become effective policy practitioners. They claim that the concepts of social capital have been part of the social work lexicon from the start of the profession, yet educators need to integrate social capital into the curriculum more effectively.

Each manuscript selected for inclusion in this book has a strong viewpoint. Each author seeks to convince us of the usefulness of using a new idea, or seeing the world in a different way. These writers force us to think about where we are, as individuals and policy practitioners, and as members of the social work profession. They point out destinations we might like to travel toward, presenting a rationale for why we might want to head that way. Agree or disagree, the process of considering our options and then choosing one is important.

Richard Hoefer

The Path to Social Justice Goes Through Politics and Economics

David Dempsey

It is time to reformulate social work policy practice theory to enhance its capacity to define more accurately the damaging problems distorting American society and to acquire appropriate intervention skills that emphasize collective action. Generous infusions of political science and economics into social work policy training, practice, and research could inform, strengthen, and provide practitioners with the cooperative action tools needed to reach their basic objectives, especially social justice.

4

Policy practice theory needs to make two crucial conceptual improve-ments: (1) integrate electoral politics fully into policy practice theory, literature, and research and (2) tie social policy training firmly to politics and economics. Current United States social welfare policy evolved from a political shift started over forty years ago with Senator Barry Goldwater's nomination as the Republican Party's 1964 presidential candidate (Perlstein, 2001). The conservatives began the takeover of the national Republican Party and their relentless march to full control of the federal government and many state governments. As conservatives acquired, accumulated, and then consolidated their power throughout the country over the next four decades, they completed many remarkable and profound changes.

An important lesson for social workers to learn from the conservative conquest and political domination is that social policy changes are rooted in politics and economics. Policy practice should be conceptually linked to politics and economics so that social workers can become innovators in contributing to a new, different political economy and a policy environ-ment conducive to fairness and equality. Changing the current social order will call for new forms of action to build both a new politics and a new economics.

Electoral politics determines who will dominate government and decides government's role. It involves much more than periodic elec-tions to choose which groups will be in charge. Politics resolves who can and does vote, which movements and organizations are influential, how groups are represented in a society's political institutions, how open or flexible political systems are to innovation, and which economic policies will be pursued. Majority politics is about running governmen-tal institutions; minority politics is about modifying, restraining, and opposing the majority. Majority politics initiates; minority politics alters or blocks.

Economic policy usually follows political change. Sustained political success brings major economic changes. Heilbroner (1985) notes: "that of necessity the political and economic realms interpenetrate in all societies" (p. 97) and that in a capitalist society:

The commanding place that economic logic assumes with respect to the gathering and disposition of surplus introduces a characteristic tension into the political nature of capitalism. For neither state nor economy can exist by itself, and each is capable, by its faulty operation, of endangering the successful operation of the other. (Heilbroner, 1985, p. 92)

The conservative swing over the past four decades has altered the economic landscape in which social workers practice and seek to influence policy. An evolving post-New Deal era social welfare policy framework has been steadily transformed into something completely different. Whereas earlier American social policy had a communal focus with solidarity and the common good as important values, the policy environment now emphasizes personal responsibility and individualism. Some have characterized the changes by using two acronyms, WITT and YOYO, which translate to "We're In This Together" and "You're On Your Own." Notice the adjustments in federal taxation, budgets, welfare, health care, Social Security, private pensions, and international trade. These conservative economic policies have completely changed the policy practice political environment.

POLITICS

What does political science have to offer to social work policy practitioners? A recent American Political Science Association (APSA) publication titled *Inequality and American Democracy,* compiled by a taskforce of the nation's most prominent political scientists, provides a stark political picture of modern America. This volume's overriding theme is an examination of the interconnections among economic and social inequalities, politics and governance, and public policies (Jacobs & Skocpol, 2005). The taskforce's central conclusions impressively reveal that the American political electorate is gravely distorted by the lack of participation in the process by between 35 and 50 percent of the eligible voters. This electoral distortion is later reflected in our governance and public policy processes, both of which function mainly to benefit the fortunate. Many distinguished political scientists examine and answer each section's major questions in the context of the discipline's research and literature. is the book contains an extensive and comprehensive bibliography.

The taskforce makes two general findings:

1. Public policy is powerfully implicated in American economic, racial, and gender inequality;
2. The effect of public policy on the political standing and capacity of citizens is at least as profound as the impact of public policies on social conditions and relationships.

The taskforce identifies five trends in policy development:

1. Direct spending programs targeted primarily toward elderly Americans have remained relatively vibrant.
2. Several forms of social provision and economic regulation targeting less advantaged non-elderly Americans have been subject to retrenchment.
3. Compared with other rich democracies, U.S. public policy has changed relatively little to reflect the changing character of the risks faced by American families as the job market and family relations have changed.
4. The period has witnessed the persistence of the 'hidden welfare state' of tax expenditures and the increasing reliance of higher-income Americans on private forms of social provision that are regulated by public policy.
5. The nature of civic participation has changed over the past three decades in ways that likely accentuate the trends just described.

If American democracy is characterized by inequality in its electorate, governance, and public policy then reversal will require mutual actions that pivot on political changes. Such changes include increasing participation through voting and electoral improvements; re-enfranchising former felons who have finished their sentences; correcting unfair census procedures; revising campaign finance practices and biased vote counting systems; creating new political parties; using multiple party nomination measures; constructing new rules for public media discourse; and lessening corporate participation in electoral politics. Social workers wanting to help shape a more humane American economy must first seek to build a fairer political system. Politics is the means to governmental authority; directing governmental institutions provides the ability to exert economic influence.

What Kind of Political Changes are Needed?

Because approximately one-half of the electorate does not vote, more political parties are needed to mobilize and include these citizens in the process. The belief that the United States is well served by having only two major political parties represented in the Congress should be abandoned. The United States, one of the world's most racially and ethnically diverse societies, has a highly stratified electorate (Zweig, 2001). Many countries with more homogenous populations have more than two political parties, offering their voters a wider spectrum of political choices. More political parties would work at informing and mustering our remarkably varied population, increase voters' choices, and perhaps encourage broader public political debate. Accommodating more political parties entails only state or federal statutory changes, not constitutional amendments.

Our political representation system could produce more diversity by replacing our "winner-take-all" style of tallying votes to a proportional representation vote-counting method. In the current system, a candidate (party) who wins by one vote wins all the political power. The candidate (party) who loses by one vote acquires next to no power. The total electorate or citizenry could be better served by a more proportional sharing of political power (Hill, 2002). Multiparty nomination ballot entries (*fusion candidates*) could also provide voters with alternatives to major party candidates. This procedure allows a candidate to be placed on the ballot line of more than one political party in the same election. For general elections, the candidate's votes on each party's ballot are added together to determine the winner (Cobble & Siskind, 1993).

Neither major political party has as a specific goal expanding the electorate. More political parties might stimulate competition to marshal greater citizen participation. Other useful institutional reforms would include easier voter registration, federal standards for national elections, including either weekend voting or designating national election day a holiday. The re-enfranchisement of felons should be a top priority. Millions of citizens, disproportionately minorities, have been permanently barred from voting by rigid laws covering convicted felons (Abramsky, 2006). Voter suppressions programs, which use legal and illegal tactics to keep certain citizens from voting and depress turnout, continue to multiply and inflict serious harm on the electoral system. "By making it more difficult to register and vote, voter-integrity rules allow politicians to modulate and control the vote" (Overton, 2006, p. 157).

Progressives need a national strategy to resist voter suppression and voter fraud programs wherever they occur and from whatever source. "The crucial question of how the nation votes in our next presidential election is unrelated to such theatrics. At issue instead is the integrity of our electoral system" (Miller, 2005, p. xi).

Building links or coalitions among existing reform groups—such as media, labor, campaign finance, prison, budget, and corporate groups pursuing separate reforms—to create a broad progressive reform movement could be a significant positive political step forward. New combined forms of political activity could bring large numbers of interested citizens together for common cause (Weil, 2005). A movement analogous to Martin Luther King's Southern Christian Leadership Conference suggests promising possibilities that could reinforce democracy and justice as well as participation and perseverance (Branch, 2006).

ECONOMICS

Although many economists have written scholarly and hard-hitting critiques of various aspects of the country's current economy, the professional economic organization has not assembled a taskforce similar to the political scientists. However, much has been published and many works provide valuable information about subjects such as income inequality (Wolff, 2002), international trade policies (Gilbert, 2004; Stiglitz, 2003), general economy (Krugman, 2003), economic thinking (Heilbroner, 1985, 1999; Warsh, 1993), politics and markets (Lindbloom, 1977), corporate reform (Ritz, 2001) and a faith-based perspective (Alford, Clark, Cortright, & Naughton, 2006). There is also important information on law and economics (Fried, 1998), income security policies (Hicks, 1999), privatization (Kahn & Minnich, 2005), capitalism (Greider, 2003; Heilbroner, 1985), tax expenditures (Howard, 1997), public assistance (Shipler, 2005), and safety nets (Pontusson, 2005).

"Economics is the study of how societies use scarce resources to produce valuable commodities and distribute them among different people" (Samuelson & Nordhaus, 2001, p. 4). Stoesz (2005, p. 67) declares that "the political economy of the United States is democratic capitalism,"which another author defines as "three dynamic and converging systems functioning as one: a democratic polity, an economy based on markets and incentives, and a moral-cultural system which is pluralistic and in the largest sense, liberal" (Novak, 1982, p. 14).

Big economic changes are necessary to orient the economy to serve the many instead of the few. The distortions identified by the political scientists in voting, governance, and public policies are mirrored in the economy. Income inequality grows and is noted more and more frequently in scholarly literature and the mainstream media (Wolff, 2002). Progressive reformers must gain control of the federal government to influence the economy. Collaborative activities that train and organize inactive citizens to become voters are crucial, as well as more vigorous participation in political and economic programs such as unions or economic cooperatives.

Changes are needed in employment policies ranging from more freedom for labor to organize to stronger job security and less outsourcing and privatization. Labor rights and collective bargaining issues are vital. Organized labor has two vital functions in a democratic society. They help workers secure better wages, benefits, and friendlier work environments and unions are important group actors in the larger society, providing countervailing institutional political power to private sector corporations and government.

Raising the minimum wage can immediately help a large segment of the poorest workers and demonstrates progressive possibilities in mutual political and economic action. Watching the 109th Congress raise its own pay while rejecting a minimum wage increase illustrates perfectly a major contemporary policy dilemma – how to address the class warfare America's wealthy wages incessantly on the middle and working classes, while the rich deny the existence of any political class warfare.

Public and private pension systems need to be reviewed and new laws and regulations developed to protect them. A national health care system is a priority. The frightening growth of government, corporate, financial, and personal debt must be curbed, reduced, and managed in a way beneficial to ordinary people. More insight is vital regarding the destructive uses of public debt to narrow society's future public policy choices.

Other essential economic changes include fairer, progressive taxes, humane budget policies, modernizing entitlement programs, different international trade arrangements, and a new safety net. Trade agreements could be renegotiated to include labor rights and worker mobility provisions as well as the ability of individuals to move freely in the trade zones. Progressive features need to be restored to federal and state corporate and income tax programs and the federal estate tax maintained. Economic cooperatives could play an important role, particularly among the working and lower classes.

Looming over America's political economy, and illustrating perfectly Heilbroner's observation about the interpenetration of political and economic realms, is the corporation and the role it plays in our society. Ritz (2001) writes that

> Corporations today act in the capacity of governments. Energy corporations determine our nation's energy policies. Automobile corporations determine our nation's transportation policies. Military manufacturing corporations determine our nation's defense policies. Corporate polluters and resource extraction corporations define our environmental policies. Transnational corporations determine our trading policies. And the wealthiest among us—with their wealth deeply rooted in corporations—determine our tax policies.

> Corporations are armed with 'free speech,' 'managerial prerogative,' 'due process,' 'equal protection,' the Commerce clause, the Contracts clause, and all the lawyers, lobbyists, and 'buy partisan' support that wealth can buy. With all this at their disposal corporate leaders increasingly define our culture, our schools, our elections, and the operations of our government itself. (p. xiv)

SOCIAL WORK/POLICY PRACTICE

Social work's basic practice paradigm is that of an individual in one's environment (*person-in-environment*), which focuses distinctly on the person (Karls & Wandrei, 1995). The paradigm has always tolerated two major anomalies in practice: (1) the focus on person has rarely included the "political person" and (2) the focus on person slights the role of institutions in peoples' lives, yet institutions such as politics, government, religion, corporations, banks, military and media are primary influences in everyone's life.

The focus on person in the paradigm usually means a sick person, or an unemployed person, or a homeless person, or a disabled person, or an addicted person, or a mentally ill person. The focus on person is rarely used to portray a politically inactive or politically powerless person. Since the paradigm also avoids the role of institutions in a person's environment, social workers seldom connect the clients' shabby treatment from institutions to the clients' political inactivity and powerlessness. There is also less inclination to consider group or shared intervention strategies.

The social work paradigm's anomalies also exist in the larger American society and need to be challenged and overcome: (1) many American citizens are not political participants, ignoring even basic political activities such as registering to vote and partaking in elections and (2) our society's basic institutions mostly benefit the advantaged.

One way to correct the paradigm's anomalies would be to adopt political and economic activities and tactics that focus on group action. Problems identified in this article call for organized activity aimed at basic societal institutions by large numbers of currently politically inactive people. The reality is that the scope and nature of the problems in today's environment are not amenable to current social work interventions. Solving these problems requires cooperative collective action; the problems lack clinical or direct practice solutions. Collective action interventions could potentially empower practitioners considerably, and clients exponentially.

The current policy practice model relies primarily on legislative lobbying for change (Midgley, Tracy, & Livermore, 1999). Frequently lobbying is the default position for practitioners engaged in advocacy for change. Lobbying is valuable and necessary in context but it is much too narrow a tool to solve these big problems. A greater value must be assigned to electoral politics. If social work wants an advocacy default position, electoral politics makes much more sense. Major social change requires the concerted political activity of large groups working cooperatively to win government control rather than just lobbying the existing government. Current policy practice training empowers practitioners but ignores client empowerment and the need for institutional reform. Policy practice overemphasizes lobbying while slighting electoral politics. Social workers tend to identify politics as lobbying for programs and issues instead of understanding it as an instrument and process for large numbers of people to realize a different society that might apply values such as solidarity, self-determination, democracy, empowerment, inclusion, participation, diversity, and social justice to establish a more equitable social order.

Social workers should embrace politics and economics because these foundational areas contain our society's biggest and most tenacious problems. These two disciplines are researching and writing copiously on these problems and can provide policy social workers with the knowledge and skills to become political innovators, a new and potent role that can transform their practice. Some perceptions of social workers are driven by the political powerlessness and marginality of their clients. Practitioners that politically empower clients will also politically empower their profession. Otherwise social workers face the prospect of being irrelevant and secondary to achieving a better social order. Through vigorous political and economic activities, social workers and clients will be able to create history instead of only reacting to current events.

A political contradiction exists in the social services community between the professionals who provide services and service users (*clients*) that is ignored. This is an unacknowledged, unidentified subject in the social and other human services. The contradiction is this: most professional providers are vigorous and effective participants in American politics, whereas many clients are not. It is a peculiar phenomenon. We help clients acquire basic economic skills such as budgeting or consumer education or debt management. We work with them in intimate areas such as marriage and family problems or parenting. However, when it comes to equipping clients with basic political skills, it is as if an *iron curtain* exists between the social work professionals and clients.

This situation needs reexamination. Talking to clients about basic political skills can occur without partisan predjudice, just as economic information can be shared without telling people to buy the blue Buick or lease the green Ford or to rent an apartment or buy a house. We can talk to clients about political values such as inclusion, participation, solidarity, and social justice and how to implement them without talking about Republicans or Democrats or Greens or Libertarians.

Because many citizens eschew political involvement, the system rewards the engaged who already benefit in our society. As the ASPA taskforce on inequality observed in its policy development trends "Direct spending programs targeted primarily toward elderly Americans have remained relatively vibrant" (Jacobs & Skocpol, 2005, p. 13) but "Several forms of social provision and economic regulation targeting less advantaged non-elderly Americans have been subject to retrenchment" (Jacobs & Skocpol, 2005, p. 13). The implications are clear. The latent political power of inactive citizens, many of whom are social work clients or recipients of other human services, must be realized and integrated into the electorate to bring balance into our system.

Electoral political participation is essential to changing the environment and its institutions. Solid knowledge about politics and economics will be key to realizing these changes. Our society is riddled with political and economic distortions that are detrimental to many citizens. Inactive citizens are basically unrepresented in American political decisions. Political participation and representation are central to the healthy functioning of American democracy. Establishing political fairness and justice depends upon an involved, invigorated electorate focused on the common good.

Social justice is a fundamental social work value and societal objective. Social workers must understand politics and economics to learn how to use democracy and the Constitution to reach an inclusive and representative electorate and to manage our free market economy for everyone's benefit (Dahl, 2001; Sunstein, 2004). Besides being society's primary foundational institutions, politics and economics naturally fosters more group and corporate activities. Electoral politics provides the only peaceful and constructive major change vehicle available to ordinary citizens. Practitioners and clients cannot achieve social justice in the American political system without involvement in politics and economics. Social work can design new intervention techniques and strategies to reform, renew, and reinvigorate our society's major institutions by applying the research and literature of politics and economics. The path to social justice in America goes through politics and economics.

REFERENCES

Abramsky, S. (2006). *Conned: How millions went to prison, lost the vote, and helped send George W. Bush to the White House.* New York: New Press.

Alford, O. P., H., Clark, C.M.A., Cortright, S. A., & Naughton, M. J. (2006). *Rediscovering abundance: Interdisciplinary essays on wealth, income, and their distribution in the Catholic social tradition.* Notre Dame, IN: University of Notre Dame Press.

Branch, T. (2006). *At Canaan's edge: America in the King years, 1965–68.* New York: Simon & Schuster.

Cobble, S., & Siskind, S. (1993). *Fusion: Multiple party nominations in the United States.* Madison, WI: The Center for a New Democracy.

Dahl, R. A. (2001). *How democratic is the American Constitution?* New Haven, CT: Yale University Press.

Fried, B. H. (1998). *The progressive assault on laissez-faire: Robert Hale and the First Law and Economic Movement.* Cambridge, MA: Harvard University Press.

Gilbert, N. (2004). *Transformation of the welfare state: The silent surrender of public responsibility.* New York: Oxford University Press.

Greider, W. (2003). *The soul of capitalism: Opening paths to a moral economy.* New York: Simon & Schuster.

Heilbroner, R. L. (1985). *The nature and logic of capitalism.* New York: W.W. Norton.

Heilbroner, R. L. (1999). *The worldly philosophers: The lives, times, and ideas of the great economic thinkers* (7th ed.). New York: Simon & Schuster.

Hicks, A. (1999). *Social democracy and welfare capitalism: A century of income security politics.* Ithaca: NY: Cornell University Press.

Hill, S. (2002). *Fixing elections: The failure of America's winner take all politics.* New York: Routledge.

Howard, C. (1997). *The hidden welfare state: Tax expenditures and social policy in the United States.* Princeton: NJ: Princeton University Press.

Jacobs, L. R., & Skocpol, T. (2005). *Inequality and American democracy: What we know and what we need to learn.* New York: Russell Sage Foundation.

Kahn, S., & Minnich, E. (2005*). The fox in the henhouse: How privatization threatens democracy.* San Francisco: Berrett-Koehler.

Karls, J., & Wandrei, K. (1995). Person-in-environment. In R. L. Edwards (Ed. inchief), *Encyclopedia of social work* (19th ed.), Vol. 3, (pp. 1819–1827). Washington, DC: NASW Press.

Krugman, P. (2003). *The great unraveling: Losing our way in the new century.* New York: W.W. Norton.

Lindbloom, C. E. (1977). *Politics and markets.* New Haven, CT: Yale University Press.

Midgley, J., Tracy, M. B., & Livermore, M. (1999). *Handbook of social policy.* Thousand Oaks, CA: Sage Publications.

Miller, M. C. (2005). *Fooled again: The real case for electoral reform.* New York: Basic Books.

Novak, M. (1982). *The spirit of democratic capitalism.* New York: American Enterprise Institute/Simon & Schuster.

Overton, S. (2006). *Stealing democracy: The new politics of voter suppression.* New York: W.W. Norton.

Perlstein, R. (2001). *Before the storm: Barry Goldwater and the unmaking of the American consensus.* New York: Hill & Wang.

Pontusson, J. (2005). *Inequality and prosperity: Social Europe vs. liberal America.* Ithaca, NY: Cornell University Press.

Ritz, D. (Ed). (2001). *Defying corporations, defining democracy: A book of history & strategy.* New York: Apex Books.

Samuelson, P. A., & Nordaus, W. D. (2001). *Economics* (17th ed.). New York: McGraw-Hill. (p. 4).

Shipler, D. K. (2005). *The working poor: Invisible in America.* New York: Vintage Books.

Stiglitz, J. E. (2003). *The roaring nineties: A new history of the world's most prosperous decade.* New York: W.W. Norton.

Stoesz, D. (2005). *Quixote's ghost: The right, the Liberati, and the future of social policy.* New York: Oxford University Press.

Sunstein, C. R. (2004). *The second Bill of Rights: FDR's unfinished revolution and why we need it more than ever.* New York: Basic Books.

Warsh, D. (1993). *Economic principals: Masters and mavericks of modern economics.* New York: Free Press.

Weil, M. (Ed.). (2005). *The handbook of community practice.* Thousand Oaks, CA: Sage Publications.

Wolff, E. N. (2002). *Top heavy: The increasing inequality of wealth in America and what can be done about it.* New York: Free Press.

Zweig, M. (2001). *The working class majority: America's best kept secret.* Ithaca, NY: ILR Press/Cornell University Press.

A Strengths-Based Framework for Social Policy: Barriers and Possibilities

Katharine Hill

A commitment to strengths-based practice lies at the very heart of social work practice. It is incorporated in the National Association of Social Workers (NASW) code of ethics, in social work education, and in practice at all levels and settings. However, the concept of a strengths-based framework for social policy development and analysis is less well developed. Is it possible to create and implement social policy that adheres to the key principles of strengths-based practice? Can a strengths-based approach be applied in the current policy climate? Traditional social policy development and analysis is driven by a problem-centered approach, often arising from a needs assessment, and evaluated on its success in addressing the social problem as it is operationalized in the policy. Although elements of a strengths perspective may be incorporated, the bias of most social policy is toward a problem-focused approach.

The practicality of bringing the values of a strengths-based approach to the forefront of the policy-making process has yet not been determined, nor has the best method for doing so been identified. In addition, the implementation of a strengths-based policy, with a focus on environmental and systemic change, remains quite challenging in an era of trying to do more with less and diminishing investment in social services. Although social policies have incorporated elements of a strengths-based approach, none have fully incorporated the theory into the reality of policy development and implementation. It may be that the best option for social workers in the policy arena is to view the strengths-based framework as one method of analysis in an arsenal of many, rather than as the only measure of a policy's success or failure.

OVERVIEW OF THE STRENGTHS PERSPECTIVE

The concept of focusing on clients' strengths is at the very core of social work values. Social workers are ethically bound to "enhance the capacity of people to address their own needs" (NASW, 1999, p. 1) through interventions at the individual, group, and community level. Strengths-based social work practice is rooted in the belief that all people have a wide range of talents, abilities, capacities, skills, resources, and aspirations. These strengths drive human growth when they are identified, recognized, and developed (Saleebey, 2006; Weick, Rapp, Sullivan, & Kirsthart, 1989). Conversely, focusing on problems and deficits in people and communities inhibits growth. Therefore, in their practice, social workers should focus on strengths to enhance growth and bring about positive change (Saleebey, 2006; Weick et al., 1989).

The strengths perspective emphasizes the construction of the social work interaction. The constructionist view places a strong emphasis on the use of symbols, icons, and words in constructing meaning of the human experience (Saleebey, 1996). The strengths approach to social work practice, whether at the micro, meso, or macro level, places the stories of the target population, their community, cultural identity, and institutions at the center of practice. The emphasis is on enhancing or building upon these pre-existing strengths, when possible, rather than building new institutions or systems to work with the population of focus. A crucial component of this approach is allowing the client to define the areas of focus for the intervention and the desired goals and outcomes of that intervention (Weick et al., 1989).

Part of the focus on social construction in a strengths-based practice is an emphasis on the importance of language, both in describing the area for work, as well as in describing the interventions that are identified by the social worker and the client. Saleebey (1996, 2006) identifies a "lexicon" of strengths, the key words and concepts that are the core values of the strengths perspective of practice. Plasticity, or the placebo effect, refers to the power of hope and of the ability of people to continually transform themselves. Empowerment recognizes the capacities of people to engage in meaningful decision making and recognize and use the tools and resources that are available to them, both internally and externally. Membership recognizes the value of community membership as a way of building strength and capacity. Resilience is the ongoing and developing fund of energy and skill that can be used in current struggles. Healing and wholeness focuses on the innate ability of humans to regenerate and resist when faced with disease or disruption. Dialogue and collaboration occurs as social worker and clients work together to identify client desires and the resources needed to meet those desires. Social workers must practice suspension of disbelief in strengths-based work. They must take clients at their word, and believe what they have to say about themselves and their reasons for desiring change (Saleebey, 1996, 2006).

Social work values provide a natural foundation for a strengths-based practice, because of its fit with the existing ethics and values of the profession. Focusing on problems makes it "difficult for practitioners to express some of the fundamental values of the profession. The belief in the dignity and worth of each individual and the corresponding belief in individual and collective strength and potential cannot be realized fully in the midst of concerns about assessing liabilities" (Weick et al., 1989, p. 352).

Despite the good fit of the strengths model with social work values, strengths theorists argue that it is a challenge for social workers to abandon the problem-solving model and focus on strengths because of the widespread acceptance of the problem-solving approach (Saleebey 2006; Weick et al., 1989). This would appear to be especially true in the application of a strengths-based approach to social policy.

TRADITIONAL SOCIAL WORK SOCIAL POLICY FRAMEWORKS

Social policy analysis and development most often begins with the problem that the policy is created to address. For example, social welfare policy in the United States is, arguably, designed to address the problem of poverty. Countless needs assessments have been completed to identify the significance of the problem of poverty, to operationalize the problem, and to determine the efficacy of various interventions at addressing the problem as it is defined. The existence of the defined social problem is the reason for the policy intervention.

Social work models for policy analysis use systematic methods to evaluate the efficacy of social policies in meeting the mission and goals of the state (Karger & Stoesz, 2006), or, in other words in "solving" the problem. Karger and Stoesz (2006) propose a model for policy analysis that begins with an examination of the historical background of the policy, including the historical problems that led to the creation of the policy. Once a historical perspective has been provided, policy analysts are instructed to move on to gaining greater understanding of the problem that necessitated the policy; how the policy is designed, financed, and implemented; and then an analysis of the feasibility, cost-effectiveness, efficiency, and congruence of the goals of the policy with its stated area of impact and change. They also discuss the importance of understanding the ideological assumptions of policy development and analysis, including gaining an understanding of the social vision, ideological assumptions, and major beneficiaries of the policy.

Karger and Stoesz (2006) specifically call for policy analysts to examine the congruence of the policy goals with the values of professional social work, but do not offer guidance as to the best ways to create policies that fit with these values. They also acknowledge that, despite the analytic framework, "social policy analysis is largely subjective" (p. 36). Reasons for subjectivity include the analyst's own value system, understanding of the policy and policy problem, and the political environment that the analysis takes place in. Their analytical framework calls for human service professionals to examine the impact of a social policy on the public good, but as the definition of this is inherently subjective, it is not always clear how to proceed with this task.

Chambers and Wedel (2005) also provide a framework for policy analysis for social workers and human service professionals. Their framework proposes that policy analysis should evaluate mission, goals, and objectives of the policy; the forms of benefits or services required; entitlement (eligibility) rules; administrative or organizational structure for service delivery; financing method; and interactions among these elements. Understanding the values of a policy and its development are key components to this framework as well. The fit of a policy element to the social problem of concern should be evaluated, as well as the consequences of each policy element with regard to adequacy, equity, and efficiency for the target population of the policy.

Chambers and Wedel (2005) describe values-infused approaches to policy analysis, ranging from value analytic to value critical to value committed. They argue that an important part of social policy analysis is the judgment of the "goodness" of a policy, whether it is just, fair, or appropriate to the target population. They differentiate between a value-analytic approach, which describes what a policy is, but does not describe what it should be: a value-committed approach, in which the analyst starts with a strongly held position of how things ought to be; and a value-critical approach, which uses value-based criteria to highlight policy programs and features. They argue that a value-critical approach is the most appropriate method of analysis for social workers, in that it forces social workers to

> analyze for multiple and competing values and frames of reference, to make hard choices among them, and take even their own frames and values into question as they confront the reality of both the social world in general, the world their clients/consumers live in, and the daily operating world of organizations, laws, and public expectations. (Chambers & Wedel, 2005, p. 52)

OVERVIEW OF STRENGTHS PERSPECTIVE OF POLICY ANALYSIS/FORMATION

A strengths-based perspective to policy analysis and formation is clearly value-based, driven by the key elements of the strengths-based social work. In the continuum created by Chambers and Wedel (2005), it is value-committed, because it is normative and seeks to change or improve the social policy environment to better meet its vision. A strengths-based approach to social policy views "people as complete human beings, creates a symbolic sense of urgency, requires attention to paradox, and expects divergent and dialectical, rather than convergent solutions" (Weick & Saleebey, 1995, p. 147). A strengths-based approach "amplifies" the strengths in community, and encourages the transfer of those strengths to areas that need support, rather than isolating the weaker areas and not acknowledging what already exists in the community that could be used to address those areas of need (Rappaport, Davidson, Wilson, & Mitchell, 1975).

Despite social work's commitment to a strengths approach, the concept is not well developed in the social policy arena. Sandler, Ayers, Suter, Schultz and Twohey-Jacobs (2004) say that social policies may promote strengths through one of four pathways: positive development, prevention of future adversities, protection from negative effects of adversities, and counteraction of the negative effects of adversities. However, a policy must reach beyond one of these pathways to be considered strengths-based.

Chapin (1995) argues that, although social policies are constructed as a public response to social problems, when "the problem is defined, the labeling process and a societal predisposition to create a social construction of reality to fit the needs of the people in power may transform people into problems" (p. 506). She does not deny the existence of social problems, but instead argues that the current system of defining the problem emphasizes people's problems, rather than acknowledging structural and environmental barriers to their success. The strengths-based policy framework draws attention to the "inconsistencies and incongruities" within a policy and within individuals' environments, which create additional barriers for success, rather than creating opportunities (Rapp, Pettus, & Goscha, 2006). Weick and Saleebey (1995) argue that social policy as it is currently implemented in the United States creates definitions that do not encompass the people's environment, nor do these definitions recognize the importance of community. A strengths-based framework seeks to address this shortcoming. Rapp, Pettus, and Goscha (2006) state "a strengths-based policy framework does not discount or disregard 'problems' or negative events in a person or community environment, but chooses to focus on what these barriers are preventing, and ways to more fully use existing resources and capacities of an individual or environment to overcome such barriers" (p. 7).

A strengths approach to social policy requires that the policymakers avoid blame in the problem definition and recognize that the definition of a problem depends on who is viewing it, and who is describing it. It creates space for dialogue and mutual definition of social problems, so that they can be conceptualized to reflect the "realities of the people who are experiencing them" (Chapin, 1995, p. 508). This is in keeping with the constructionist approach inherent in the strengths approach to practice. It recognizes the importance of language in the construction of intervention, and the necessity of incorporating the viewpoints and experiences of the people who undergo and survive the social problems, rather than depending on experts to define the problem and create the boundaries of the intervention.

A strengths-based approach to public policy expands the role of the target population of the policy by actively seeking to include them in the policy-making process, from conceptualization, through implementation, to evaluation. An effective policy developer "gives voice to clients' perspectives, helps negotiate definitions and goals that include these perspectives, and continues to focus on client as collaborator throughout the evaluation phase" (Chapin, 1995, p. 510), rather than acting as the all-knowing professional or expert.

Key components of a strengths-based policy framework include the following:

- The policy-making process is open and inclusive of the target populations of the policy, including both social workers and the direct beneficiaries of the policy (Chapin, 1995).
- Policy decisions are shaped by normative-affective as well as logical-empirical factors. Including the "targets" of a policy in the policy-making process will create emotional connections with policymakers which will lead to policies that are more supportive of their beneficiaries (Chapin, 1995).
- Social policies start with a goal statement, and the problem is defined as the barrier(s) to achieving that goal (Rapp et al., 2006).
- Traditional social policy begins with a definition of the social problem, assessment, extent, and exact nature of the problem. This easily shifts to blaming the victim, because the assessment focuses on what is wrong with those affected by the problem and why they are different from the rest of the population. Strengths-based social policy begins with the "strengths, competencies and resources needed for preventing or dealing with adversities rather than the

deficits, pathologies and deviance that can result from them" (Leadbeater, Schellenbach, Maton, & Dodgen, 2004, p. 25).

- The goal of a social policy should be defined by the target population that is directly impacted by the potential policy, so that the goal is congruent with that population's experience (Rapp et al., 2006). The goals of the policy should recognize the diversity of responses to a social problem, rather than trying to create a generalized response that can be applied to all people and communities in the targeted situations (Leadbeater et al., 2004).

- Strengths-based social policy should be voluntary for the beneficiaries, and emphasize their right to choose the services that they wish to access. Policies should not be coercive "because the intent of a strengths-based policy is to create opportunities for persons to use their strengths, talents, and skills to meet a desired goal" (Rapp et al., 2006, p. 10).

- Strengths-based social policy emphasizes equal membership and a positive perception of the environment. Existing and "natural" community resources should be utilized by the targeted group, rather than developing segregated services to address a specific problem, which inherently segregate the population that uses them (Chapin, 1995; Rapp et al., 2006). The policy should be collaborative, focusing on the interrelationships among individuals, families, groups and communities in their response to adversities, rather than on the individual's response (Leadbeater et al., 1994).

- Strengths-based social policy recognizes the long-term approaches and responses that communities and individuals develop to respond to adversities, rather than their short-term response to crises (Leadbeater et al., 2004).

- Evaluation of policies' effectiveness should reflect the ideas of the people who are most clearly affected by it and the outcomes that can be expected to result (Chapin, 1995).

- Strengths-based social policy rewards successes; it does not just punish failures. Programs and services that are successful in helping target beneficiaries achieve their desired goals should be rewarded (Rapp et al., 2006). The policy places the onus for success on the service provider and social system, not just on the target group or individual.

Clearly, a strengths-based policy framework is a value-committed approach to social policy formation and analysis. Rapp et al. (2006) point out that, although the strengths-based approach to policy analysis is value-driven, it "does not make the myriad of trade-offs imbedded in any policy disappear. To get one principle you might have to sacrifice another" (p. 15). This is perhaps where the challenge lies—how many trade-offs can be made before the identity of a policy as "strengths-based" is lost?

YOUTH POLICY AND THE STRENGTHS PERSPECTIVE

A substantial body of literature demonstrates the value of a strengths-based approach (also called resiliency or youth development approach, among others) to work with children and adolescents (Furstenberg, Cook, Eccles, Elder, & Sameroff, 1999; Stein 2005). However, it is unclear if this approach stretches to the social welfare policy that directs so much of the youth work. Individual caseworkers or programs may approach their work from a strengths perspective, focusing on the resiliencies and abilities of the youth whom they work with, but is it possible to apply this same approach in social policy development and analysis?

A case in point is the John H. Chafee Foster Care Independence Act. Passed in 1999, the Chafee Act expanded federal funding for independent living services for youth transitioning from foster care. The Chafee Act funds can be used to offer youth education, vocational, and employment training, including special help for youth ages 18 to 21 who have aged out of foster care. The Chafee Act was amended to include the Educational and Training Voucher Program (ETVP) in 2001. The ETVP authorized $60 million for payments to states for educational and training vouchers for youth participating in postsecondary education and vocational programs (National Foster Care Coalition, 2005). The Chafee Act contains specific language referring to the need to provide "personal and emotional support to children aging out of foster care, through mentors and the promotion of interactions with dedicated adults" (National Foster Care Coalition 2005, p. 47). I selected the Chafee Act for this analysis for several reasons. First, because of the focus in youth work and youth research on affirmative, strengths-based approaches to practice, it is logical to apply the same principles to youth-based public policy. Second, the legislation recognizes the importance of at least some strengths-based approaches to work with youth, such as mentoring and relationships with caring adults. Third, Chafee does seem to seek to provide "amplifiers" to youths' strengths, through its emphasis on the provision of training and education for youth transitioning out of care. Fourth, it attempts to address strengths of youth through all four of Sandler et al.'s (2004) pathways:

1. it focuses on positive development of youth transitioning from care;
2. it tries to prevent the occurrence of future adversities by providing youth with tools for a more successful adult life;
3. it tries to protect youth from the negative effects of past adversities by creating additional supports, such as education and training funding or independent living programs; and
4. it counteracts some of the negative effects of adversities by promoting the development of additional competencies in the targeted youth.

Finally, for the sake of this analysis, the Chafee program is a relatively contained program. It is an easy policy to analyze due to its clearly stated and limited target population, problem, and intervention.

DOES THE CHAFEE ACT MEET THE PRINCIPLES OF STRENGTHS-BASED SOCIAL POLICY?

The Chafee Act meets some, but not all of the principles of strengths-based social policy, as are delineated in the principles developed by Chapin (1995), Leadbeater et al. (2004), and Rapp, Patus, and Goscha (2006). Its initial development included advocates and social workers. Policymakers were introduced to foster youth and heard their stories and experiences, thus creating an emotional connection with the "problem" (National Foster Care Coalition, 2005). The Chafee Act includes specific language calling for foster youth involvement in the implementation of the Act, through youth boards or councils, as well as in their own service planning and delivery (National Foster Care Awareness Project, 2000). Youth participation in Chafee programs is voluntary, and they can select, within certain parameters, how the funds are utilized—what kind of training they receive, where they attend school, and where they live. In this way, the program attempts to recognize the diversity of experiences of the youth it is trying to serve. However, because the goals are set by the policy, rather than by the youth its programs are serving, it may not truly encompass the diversity of experiences and goals of youth who are transitioning from care. Finally, Chafee programs are specifically mandated to work collaboratively with other service structures and systems within the adolescent's life—a clear recognition of the interrelatedness of the responses to a young person's transition.

In other respects, the Act does not meet the principles of strengths-based policy. It starts with a problem statement, explaining the many barriers faced by youth as they age out of foster care, rather than a goal statement. It is not clear that foster youth were directly involved in the development of the policy, or in identifying the goals for their outcomes, although the goals in the policy are in keeping with the goals identified by this youth population in other studies (Collins, 2001). As mentioned previously, The Act calls for collaboration among the various youth service systems (such as juvenile justice or school-to-work programs), but does not recognize the existence or importance of more informal support networks, such as foster parents, family, friends, and community agencies. It includes specific outcomes for evaluation, but these outcomes are clearly those that are important to policymakers, with a heavy emphasis on statistics, costs, and benefits, rather than those that might be identified by former foster youth. Finally, the Chafee Act does not offer an incentive for states that are particularly successful in meeting its goals, although it also does not include a punishment for failure to meet its goals. The funds are simply made available, and states can chose to access them.

WHAT WOULD A STRENGTHS-BASED TRANSITION POLICY FOR YOUTH AGING OUT OF FOSTER CARE LOOK LIKE?

Ideally, a strengths-based transition policy for youth aging out of foster care would involve members of its target population in meaningful and ongoing development. The goals of the policy would be developed with significant input from the youth, and the interventions identified by the policy would directly address the barriers that prevent youth transitioning from foster care from meeting those goals.

A strengths-based approach "seeks to illuminate and understand the individual and environmental characteristics and protective processes that create and support developmental outcomes" (Leadbeater et al., 2004, p. 13). Barriers experienced by the youth would be viewed as coming from a poor fit between the youth and their environment, rather than with the individual youth (Furstenberg et al., 1999). As such, interventions would be focused on changing the environment to make it more inclusive of youth aging out of care, rather than on changing the individual. For example, if youth identified completing postsecondary education as a goal for transition, then the policy would directly address barriers to youth reaching this goal, such as financing education, providing ongoing educational supports (tutoring), and helping institutions of postsecondary education determine the best way to meet their needs.

As with Chafee, the participation in the programs funded by the policy would be purely voluntary for the youth, and they would be able to decide for themselves in what capacity they chose to participate. The policy would place an emphasis on the existing and "natural" community resources available to youth aging out of foster care, rather than developing segregated services solely for these youth. Providers of existing services might require extra education and training to make their services more accessible and appropriate for those aging out of foster care. For example, academic support services at colleges and universities could be tailored to address gaps in secondary education due to frequent moves. The role of the community as a "co-socializer" of youth (Furstenberg et al., 1999, p. 18) would be recognized and amplified, rather than ignored.

Finally, the goals of the policy would include building resiliency, relationship, and attachment, rather than solely focusing on attendance in school or employment. Strengths-based work places a premium on relationships; the policy would need to recognize this fact. Foster placements that allowed youth to achieve stability in their placements so that they could develop positive self-identity and self-efficacy (Stein, 2005) would be rewarded for their success. Youth would have ongoing opportunities to develop new competencies through formal and informal channels and supports. Adequate resources would be allocated to support these positive community assets (Furstenberg et al., 1999). Evaluation of the policy's efficacy would focus on the achievement of the goals identified by the youth rather than by the policymakers. The focus would shift from amelioration of the problem to achievement of goals.

IS A STRENGTHS-BASED SOCIAL POLICY FRAMEWORK PRACTICALLY FEASIBLE?

Analysis of the Chafee Act using a strengths-based perspective demonstrates that it is possible to incorporate elements of a strengths-based approach into public policy. However, it seems less likely that the framework as delineated by Chapin (1995) and by Rapp et al. (2006) could be practical for all social policy development and analysis. It seems more likely that the strengths-based policy framework could be used as a "wish list" for policy development and analysis, brought to the table by social workers to advocate for clients' goals, as well as criteria for identifying inclusion of these clients in policy development. Social workers can use the strengths-based approach to "gut check" policies, to identify specific areas for improvement or change. The process of developing and implementing policy is fraught with compromise and entails working across multiple value streams; it seems unlikely that the values of the strengths-based perspective would emerge unscathed from the negotiations necessary to create social policy. However, by keeping a strength-based approach front and center, it is possible that fewer trade-offs identified by Rapp et al. (2006) would be made without careful consideration of their impact on clients. Including the voice of the target population in the development of social policy, building on assets and community strengths, and creating policies driven by goals rather than problems, would dramatically shape the way public policies are designed and implemented.

OBSTACLES AND OPPORTUNITIES FOR A STRENGTHS-BASED APPROACH

Social workers who wish to apply a strengths-based approach to the development, implementation, and analysis of social policy may encounter obstacles and barriers from policymakers and stakeholders. Whenever a new approach is introduced, objections and concerns arise. Obstacles specific to a strengths-based approach may include:

Time. Including all the social policy stakeholders in planning and development can be a difficult and arduous task. Often, stakeholders are not versed in the policy process, are unwilling or unable to participate during "business hours," and have conflicting ideas and viewpoints with policymakers and one another. Creating meaningful opportunities for hearing stakeholders' voices takes commitment far beyond what many policymakers envisioned when they first began to develop the legislation under consideration.

Fear of change. The strengths-based approach to social policy development and analysis is different from the the usual approach. It requires that everyone involved, including policymakers, social workers, and the target

population, step outside of their usual roles and come together collaboratively and collectively to create real opportunities for social change
and development. Many participants are reluctant to commit to such a
frightening process.

Turf. A collaborative approach, drawing the resources and relationships
of stakeholders from multiple departments and communities can require
people and organizations to give up some of their hard-won area of expertise and cede control of elements of their work to others. In a tight political and economic climate, it is difficult to convince an organization to
give up part of its budget, its staff time, and its control to create opportunities that may not be successful.

A Long-Term Approach to Change is not Popluar. Often, public policy
is created in response to a crisis that seems to demand an immediate
response and solution. If the response instead focuses on sustainable,
long-term, multigenerational change, it may be viewed as too expensive,
too ineffective, and not immediate enough.

Skepticism. The strengths-based approach to practice is often dismissed
as "Pollyanna-ism" or "just language" rather than meaningful change.
Perhaps attempts to create policy that involves all stakeholders, is based
in relationships, and amplifies strengths may be marginalized or less
respected than they deserve, because the power of a strengths-based
approach is not universally recognized.

Despite these challenges, some areas of a strengths-based approach to
social policy provide real opportunities for application in the policy-making arena. These opportunities may provide a window into the policy-
making discussion for social workers to advocate a strengths-based
approach to policy work.

1. In times of financial pressures, limited budgets, and time constraints,
   the concept of collaboration and sharing resources, budgets, and time
   can be very popular. The strengths-based approach to policy development and implementation-specific focus on building relationships,
   identifying informal supports and networks, and amplifying existing
   resources can be framed to be politically pleasing.
2. Rewarding programs and practitioners for their successes is already
   included in the political lexicon. The challenge for a strengths-based
   approach lies in the definition of success, in creating a definition of
   success that is broad enough to incorporate the diversity of experience,

goals, and progress that is the crux of strengths-based practice. This may be difficult in an era of accountability and standardized testing, but certainly is possible.

3. The strengths-based approach is effective. For example, research has demonstrated that early intervention programs for children lead to greater success in their adolescence (Sandler et al., 2004). Policymakers are committed to providing good outcomes for their constituents. As research continues to demonstrate the effectiveness of strengths-based approaches to social policy, policymakers will be more likely to create and implement such approaches.

CONCLUSIONS

To truly change the policy-making process to a strengths-based approach a sea change must occur at all levels of government. The focus needs to shift from political interests and financial concerns to creating and sustaining human dignity and opportunity for all citizens in the face of adversity. Chambers and Wedel (2005) point out that when using a value-committed approach to policy development, "the policy discourse will then not be about operating details of policies and programs, but about more fundamental social and structural problems" (p. 50). The focus shifts from the details and pragmatic concerns of a social policy to addressing the systemic and environmental barriers faced by youth as they transition from care. A strengths-based framework for social policy development and analysis, although perhaps not practically feasible at this time when used as the sole method for social policy development and analysis, is an appropriate and important tool for social workers and advocates as they try to improve outcomes for their clients.Furthermore, it can be a powerful tool for advocating for improvements in social policy, thus recognizing the human dignity and value of all of all citizens.

REFERENCES

Chambers, D., & Wedel, K. (2005). *Social policy and social programs: A method for the practical public policy analyst* (4th ed.). Boston: Pearson Education.

Chapin, R. (1995). Social policy development: The strengths perspective. *Social Work* *40*(4), 506–514.

Collins, M. (2001). Transition to adulthood for vulnerable youths: A review of research and implications for policy. *Social Service Review, 75*(2), 272–291.

Furstenberg, F., Cook, T., Eccles, J., Elder, G., & Sameroff, A. (1999). *Managing to make it: Urban families and adolescent success.* London: University of Chicago Press.

Karger, H., & Stoesz, D. (2006). *American social welfare policy: A pluralist approach.* Boston: Pearson Education.

Leadbeater, B., Schellenbach, C., Maton, K., & Dodgen, D. (2004). Research and policy for building strengths: Processes and contexts of individual, family, and community development. In Maton, K., Schellenbach, C., Leadbeater, B., & Solarz, A. (Eds.). *Investing in children, youth, families, and communities: Strengths-based research and policy* (pp. 13–30). Washington, DC: American Psychological Association.

National Association of Social Workers (1999). *Code of Ethics of the National Association of Social Workers.* Retrieved July 25, 2007 from: http://www.socialworkers.org/pubs/code.

National Foster Care Awareness Project (2000). *Frequently asked questions II about the Foster Care Independence Act of 1999 and the John H. Chafee Foster Care Independence Program.* Washington, DC: Author.

National Foster Care Coalition. (2005). *Frequently asked questions III about the Chafee Foster Care Independence Program and the Chafee Educational and Training Voucher Program.* Washington, DC: Author.

Rapp, C., Pettus, C., & Goscha, R. (2006). Principles of strengths-based policy. *Journal of Policy Practice, 5*(4), 3–18.

Rappaport, J., Davidson, W., Wilson, M., & Mitchell, A. (1975). Alternative to blaming the victim or the environment: Our places to stand have not moved the earth. *American Psychologist, 30*(4), 525–528.

Saleebey, D. (1996). The strengths perspective in social work practice: Extensions and cautions. *Social Work, 41*(3), 296–305.

Saleebey, D. (2006). *The strengths perspective in social work practice* (4th ed.) Boston: Pearson Education.

Sandler, I., Ayers, T., Suter, J., Schultz, A., & Twohey-Jacobs, J. (2004). Adversities, strengths and public policy. In Maton, K., Schellenbach, C., Leadbetter, B., & Solarz, A. (Eds.). *Investing in children, youth, families, and communities: Strengths-based research and policy* (pp. 31–49). Washington, DC: American Psychological Association.

Stein, M. (2005). Young people aging out of care: The poverty of theory. *Children and Youth Services Review, 28*(4), 422–434.

Weick, A., Rapp, C., Sullivan, P., & Kisthardt, W. (1989). A strengths perspective for social work practice. *Social Work, 34*(4), 350–354.

Weick, A. & Saleebey, D. (1995). Supporting family strengths: Orienting policy and practice toward the 21st century. *Families in Society: The Journal of Contemporary Human Services, 76*(3), 141–149.

Bridging the Divide Between Community Organizing Efforts and Direct Services in Traditional Social Service Agencies: Lessons Learned from a Case Study

Eli Bartle
Beth Halaas

INTRODUCTION

Recently, the social work profession as a whole has not had a visible presence in activist and community organizing efforts, including workplace and wage-reform movements. Although social work has a rich background of both labor history and social change activity, the profession does not appear to offer real-life models of organizations or institutions that reflect such community organizing efforts within the traditional social service delivery systems. This contradiction between social work's focus on poverty and public welfare policy and the absence of social work and social service agencies from activist movements leads to an important query. Questions leading from this query include Why aren't social welfare agencies consistently named as supporters of activist efforts? What involvement do social service agencies have in community organizing efforts? What encourages or inhibits this involvement? In an effort to explore social service agencies, and specifically, social work professionals' participation or lack of participation within the agencies, in community organization efforts, a case study was conducted using the living wage campaign in a large U.S. city.

Typically (and even more so in recent years), social service agencies focus on providing direct services to individuals and families and have limited time to focus on community organization efforts. On the other hand, social work policy texts now include a discussion of one of the economic survival strategies and community organizing campaigns to relieve poverty for people in the low-wage labor market: the living wage movement. (See Jansson, 2003 and Karger & Stoesz, 2006.) As a community organizing effort, this movement offers incremental reform of the labor market by calling for an adequate wage plus benefits for direct government workers and anyone who works for a government contractor or corporation that receives assistance from that government. Through 2006, 130 cities, counties, and/or educational institutions have passed living wage ordinances and at least another 110 coalitions of community, religious, and union organizations are currently working to pass living wage laws and policies, including 20 state campaigns (Living Wage Campaign, 2006). Each ordinance is tailored to meet the specific needs of the community, and, unlike the minimum wage, strives to raise workers' salaries so that they are equal to or above the federal poverty guideline (Karger & Stoesz, 2006). Social service agencies and social work professionals are *not* commonly named as active participants in the living wage movement. Instead, primarily churches and labor unions are credited with starting, sustaining, and supporting this movement (Living Wage Resource Center, 2005).

Due to descriptions of the various living wage campaigns as examples of community policy practice in social work policy texts, the authors supposed that social workers and social service agencies would readily endorse living wage movements. Participation in one city's living wage coalition and simultaneous interviews with selected living wage movement leaders in the United States soon revealed another story. This paper will convey part of that story. In addition, the authors suggest an approach to increasing social service agency involvement in social movements and community organizing.

LITERATURE REVIEW

Social workers have always struggled to define our mission and the related practice demands: between containment and social change; maintaining the status quo or focusing on progressive activism (Abramovitz, 1996); balancing the micro, mezzo, and macro aspects of practice; providing direct casework services as well as community organizing and political lobbying services; advocating for the poor in the community via casework or providing psychotherapy (Specht & Courtney, 1994), and providing social services without losing organizing and militant focus (Brooks, 2005). Traditional social work agencies have always struggled to balance these many demands, usually by moving the focus in one direction at the expense of a focus in the other direction.

However, these demands have become more pronounced and harder to balance due, in part, to the effects of welfare reform. The dramatic shift in public welfare assistance, since the passage of the Personal Responsibility and Work Opportunity Reconciliation Act (PRWORA) of 1996, has dismantled the safety net for poor families, forcing both current and former participants into low-wage jobs. In addition, the federal government has given more decision-making power to state and local governments and to the private sector. Because of this public welfare policy change and the move toward privatization, concerns with ending poverty must increasingly focus on the labor market, the private sector, and local community groups. At the same time, social service agencies are serving individuals and families who need more economic assistance and social support to make ends meet, thus affecting the agencies' ability to address social change and the related community support efforts, generally referred to as macro issues. Thus, the dilemma: how can social service agencies provide direct services to clients as well as the necessary community organizing needed in today's times?

A review of the community organizing models does not suggest an answer to this dilemma for direct social service agencies. Approaches to community organizing efforts were historically examined using three models of community intervention: locality development, social planning policy, and social action. These strategic models, initially outlined by Rothman in the 1960s, were revised in 1996 to reflect the political, economic, and policy changes in the intervening decades. Locality development and social action are goal-oriented approaches that focus more on the community residents through self-help or shifting power relations to benefit the victims of community problems, respectively. The social work practitioner's role is an enabler-catalyst to achieve consensus among the citizens of the community or an activist advocate/agitator to affect change to benefit oppressed community residents. The social planning policy approach is task-oriented and involves both the community resident and the social work practitioner working together to solve problems—an approach that might most closely apply to direct social service agencies. The social work practitioner's role is to gather data and implement the program of community change. Rothman's (1996) updated version of these models noted that even as ideal types, they overlap in many areas. However, Rothman discusses these models as overlapping instead of as three distinct models and provides examples of organizations that fit the traditional three distinct types as well as organizations that fit the combination types. He includes feminist organizing only in the overlapping of the locality development and social action model.

Hyde (1996) critiqued Rothman's updated version of the models, arguing that although Rothman brought in the feminist perspective, he still viewed the social planning policy approach as outside of feminism. Hyde states the models should be tailored to fit the organization and the cause, and provides examples of organizations that fit combinations of all models. Hyde notes that the "field is replete with examples that confound mobilization process with organizational types" (p. 141) and calls for adding commitment and social movement focus toward understanding community intervention.

However, neither Hyde nor Rothman include any social service agencies as examples of organizations or agencies that fit their respective revised models. Rothman provides twelve examples of specific and generic organizations that fit his revised community organizing model types with feminist organizing as one type; Hyde provides 24 examples of feminist organizations that fit her revised community intervention types. None of the combined 36 examples is a social service agency. Thus, this research asks In what ways, if any, do traditional social service agencies (those that primarily provide direct services) participate in community organization efforts?

LIVING WAGE MOVEMENT AS A CASE EXAMPLE

The main supporter of living wage ordinances is the Association of Community Organizations for Reform Now (ACORN). ACORN is "the nation's largest community organization of low- and moderate-income families, working together for social justice and stronger communities" (see www.acorn.org). This social justice movement grew out of the National Welfare Rights Organization that fought for welfare reform in the 1960s (ACORN, 2005) and was composed of mostly poor black women who demanded welfare rights such as a living wage and greater access to education (Amott, 1990). Although living wage campaigns are individualized based on the local communities' needs and represented by individuals and disconnected organizations at the grassroots level, some groups have emerged consistently as identified leaders of all living wage movements. Along with ACORN, the other consistent supporters of the living wage movements are labor unions, labor-community coalitions (such as Jobs for Justice), and religious or congregation-based organizations (Luce, 2004). Noticeably absent from named supporters are social service agencies and social work professional organizations.

METHODOLOGY

Data were collected via two methods: participant observation during field research and telephone surveys. Participant observation involved becoming an active member of a newly formed living wage coalition, taking on tasks while observing the process of forming the coalition, including working with the national living wage office in Washington, DC. Field research involves "learning about, understanding, or describing a group of interacting people" (Kreuger & Neuman, 2006, p. 357). In this research, the positivist notion that contends that research is value-neutral and objective, and the idea of researcher as expert was discarded. Instead, the researcher adopted some aspects of participatory action research, a research strategy that emerged to counteract the exploitation and oppression of the subjects of the research and the withholding of knowledge from them. Engaging in participatory action research calls for the following actions:

1. understanding as well as taking action to change the situation discovered during the research process,
2. participation of the research participants in the planning and action stages,
3. an emphasis on qualitative as well as quantitative methods that might be considered traditionally 'unscientific' in classic research models,
4. collective analysis of a situation, and
5. an educational experience for those engaged in the research. (Tandon, 1981)

This research project did not use participatory action research methods in the sense that the results provided in this paper were used to inform the work of the coalition. Rather, the information was used to inform the researchers about social service agencies' levels of participation in living wage campaigns; it was not directly used to change strategies or tactics of the campaign.

The research was conducted in a large U.S. city that was just beginning its living wage campaign in fall 2003. As an active member of the living wage coalition (consisting of ACORN leaders and union members), the lead author participated in monthly meetings and conducted research on city jobs, contracts, and tax incentives to discover (1) the number of local jobs paying below a living wage and (2) the number and kind of local contracts and tax incentives with private businesses that paid below a living wage. In addition, the researcher was active in (1) the coalition that met with individual city council members to make the movement visible and to assess each council member's stance on passage of a living wage ordinance, (2) a poverty forum to increase community awareness and support, and (3) meetings with social service agencies to elicit their support and endorsements. Individually, the researcher did the following:

1. conducted telephone surveys and prepared a report concerning wages paid by city contractors;
2. interviewed contacts in successful living wage campaigns in five cities across the United States;

3. conducted a workshop with a national living wage advocate on how to start a living wage campaign;
4. participated in informal discussions with other coalition members concerning social work involvement in living wage campaigns and with students in a social work graduate policy course taught during this same time period; and
5. consulted with a national welfare Listserve concerning this issue (in an effort to formulate questions for the interviewees).

In conclusion, the researcher worked with two local social service groups, one agency and one advocacy group, both individually and with other coalition members to assess their willingness to endorse the proposed living wage ordinance and participate in the living wage movement in any other way. Both agencies had paid professional social workers on staff. All of these efforts provided data sources for this research.

For the interviews with other successful living wage campaigns, a sample of nine living wage campaigns was obtained through recommendations from the Director of ACORN's Living Wage Resource Center. Five living wage ordinance leaders or managers were interviewed. (The other four leaders declined an interview but provided referrals; all referrals were to the five living wage ordinance leaders/managers already interviewed.) Criteria for inclusion in this sample of nine were threefold:

1. The living wage campaign was likely to have social service agency involvement that ranged from a little to a lot;
2. Campaign organizers were especially active and articulate; and
3. Campaigns occurred in different areas of the United States.

The campaign contacts (i.e., managers) were e-mailed a cover letter with the questions included and asked to schedule a phone interview. The questions developed from conversations with local campaign members and social work colleagues; all questions pertained to their local living wage campaign. The questions were How were (or are) social service agencies involved in your living wage campaign? What and how many social service agencies endorsed the living wage campaign? How did social service agencies contribute? Why do you think social service agencies do or do not participate in living wage campaigns? Did the actual Living Wage Ordinance deal with social service agencies in some way and, if so, how? It is important to note that respondents to these questions included not only these five interviewees but also local and national living wage organizers as well as social workers from the Listserve and in the local community in which this case example took place.

RESULTS

Results indicate that social service agencies and the social work professionals working in these agencies are very unlikely to be directly involved in living wage campaigns but at the same time, they rarely work against living wage ordinances. Paradoxically, remaining neutral and not actively opposing living wage ordinances is a difficult task in light of threats of economic losses to their agencies from the business community. Indirect involvement is more common.

On the other hand, grassroots organizations, which are related yet different from social service agencies, do actively participate in living wage campaigns. The grassroots organizations mentioned by living wage campaign managers included coalitions for immigrant and refugee rights, community food banks, women's religious group networks, peace and justice faith-based committees, poverty and welfare rights groups, human service coalitions, and interfaith organizations. Although these organizations may on occasion employ a professionallytrained social worker, they are less likely to have professional social workers on staff. They frequently operate largely on volunteer labor.

DIRECT INVOLVEMENT: ACTIVE PARTICIPATION, REMAINING NEUTRAL, OR OPPOSITION

Traditional social service agencies (ones that employ professionallytrained social workers and have low-paying entry-level positions that may not pay a living wage) are still more prevalent than the literature indicates; they are just not always visible. Visible or active participation includes signing public endorsement lists, making public statements that the agency supports the passage of a living wage ordinance in the form of press releases, speaking at forums sponsored by the living wage coalition, and making other public statements concerning agency support. Because labor unions are active in living wage campaigns, active participation by social service agencies also indicates alignment and solidarity with union organizers. This union alignment plus the low paying entry-level positions in these agencies explains two factors that prevent social service agencies from publicly endorsing and actively participating in living wage campaigns.

Although an exception to the rule, a few traditional social service agencies do sometimes actively participate in living wage campaigns. Catholic, Lutheran, and Presbyterian social services agencies did participate directly in living wage campaigns. For example, in one city, social service agencies became involved in the debate as to whether the living wage ordinance should exempt any nonprofit social service agencies from paying living wages if the ordinance passed. In the beginning of the campaign, they were not exempt; thus, they sided with the business community and did not support a living wage ordinance because agency representatives said they could not pay higher wages unless they received more money. At approximately the same time, local unions decided to try to help the nonprofit organizations unionize. In some social service agencies, a strong relationship began to develop between unions and social service providers who had decided to unionize. Once the living wage ordinance changed to exempt nonprofit organizations from compliance, the social service agencies that had unionized, or were in the process of unionizing, actively supported the living wage campaign.

Respondents also described nonprofit social service agencies' endorsement and involvement in living wage campaigns as neutral. One respondent emphasized that it was very difficult to remain neutral in the face of threats to funding. He suspected that this was a national issue that affects many living wage campaigns and explains why social service agencies do not get involved. Three respondents indicated that the local United Way had been threatened by business leaders either directly or indirectly and had remained neutral even in the face of these threats. They were clear that remaining neutral (versus speaking out against living wage ordinances) can be, and in some instances is, a political stance because it is extremely difficult. For example, in one city business leaders first threatened social service agencies, implying that they would cut the agencies' funds mainly through United Way if the agencies actively supported the living wage campaign. Then the business leaders threatened the United Way. This information was all "secondhand," but individuals told living wage campaign leaders that in some cities business leaders had gone directly to United Way board members and made statements such as "Why should we help you when you are hurting us?" and "Gee, it would be too bad if this living wage ordinance passes and hurts businesses." In part, interviewees speculated that this neutral stance might have been due to the activists in the agency. These activists most likely spoke up informally within the agencies and found other means of expressing formal support such as through their local churches that did actively support the living wage campaign.

A second example further supports the contention that pressure from business leaders may silence social service agencies and hinder their active participation. In this particular city, administrative heads of several local social service agencies initially gave strong public support to the living wage campaign. Some spoke publicly before the city commission, joined other coalition members on radio programs, and allowed the living wage campaign leaders to use their agency's name publicly in endorsements. However, within one year, all of them had retracted their endorsement or refused any formal affiliation with the living wage campaign. Their initial support was motivated by awareness of the impact of low wages on their clientele. They withdrew public support due to pressure from those in the business community who sat on agency boards, or from wealthy donors who threatened to withdraw their financial support. In one case, United Way, under advice from business donors, withdrew from sponsoring a local program on poverty because it would have included a discussion of the living wage idea. This city's ordinance did exclude local social service agencies with less than ten employees but it included large nonprofit agencies that received public support.

Opposition to a living wage movement, although rare, occurred in the city described previously where many social service agencies initially supported a living wage movement and then later withdrew their support due to threats from business leaders. One agency in that community refused to join other agencies that initially supported the campaign because they were concerned that a living wage would raise their wage expenses. A more visible example of opposition occurred in another city in which Planned Parenthood had signed the endorsement list. The local Catholic Social Service agency was asked for an endorsement after Planned Parenthood and other prochoice organizations endorsed the campaign. When the local Catholic Social Services agency was asked to endorse the campaign, administrators asked for a copy of the current list of endorsers and when they saw the prochoice organizations on the list, they declined to endorse the campaign. The respondent speculated that perhaps if the living wage campaign had sought Catholic Social Services support prior to seeking Planned Parenthood support, Catholic Social Services would not only have actively supported the campaign but would have been less likely to withdraw their support after the fact.

INDIRECT INVOLVEMENT: INDIVIDUAL
AND AGENCY SUPPORT

All of the respondents indicated that individuals within social service organizations were active supporters of a living wage campaign, albeit in an indirect way. This within-agency support was garnered by workers in grassroots organizations that endorsed passage of the living wage ordinance. The grassroots workers networked with professional social workers in traditional agencies. They provided information about the living wage campaign and the professionals signed the endorsement list.

Sometimes these professionals helped with the living wage movement by recruiting people (both agency employees and clients) to attend events, helping with fundraising, and putting out the word. For example, a common method of garnering agency support used by living wage campaign members was to print postcards and, after receiving agency approval, put them in the waiting rooms of a social service agency. The cards were to be filled out and eventually given to the local council members. Instead of being mailed directly to the council members, the cards were returned by the agency or mailed by the client to the living wage campaign office. Clients were asked to sign the cards and to indicate in a check box if they would be willing to tell their stories, anonymously if they so chose (either in writing or by personal interview). The organizers could use the stories at the next rally, hearing, or any event in which the living wage ordinance was discussed. Clients also were asked if they wanted to get involved politically in the campaign. If clients checked this box and provided a phone number, campaign representatives would call and ask the person to testify at a poverty forum or a living wage campaign event. Cards were returned to the living wage campaign office, sorted by district, and mailed in masse to the council member representing those districts. Mailing them all at once is a tactic to show the council member how many people from his or her district are in support of a living wage. One interview respondent stated that this postcard method was the most important way to get social service agencies involved in the living wage campaign. Why? This respondent believed it was possible to get social service organizations more directly involved; however, she felt that the lack of involvement was not due to the agency, but because she did not have the time, energy, and staff to develop connections with them.

Agencies with board of directors that had decided against endorsement of a living wage ordinance still remained involved in the living wage movement. For example, an organizer in the city where social service

agencies withdrew their initial support after receiving threats by the business community members stated that many social service agencies
remained willing to contribute data and information about their clientele,
which the campaign used to educate the public on local poverty issues.

In some instances, agencies with boards of directors that had not yet
discussed the issue of endorsement were still willing to provide other
types of indirect support for a living wage ordinance. For example, in the
city where this researcher participated in the living wage campaign, one
social service agency was willing to meet with some members of the living wage coalition but made no promises concerning endorsements at the
end of that meeting. She indicated that she might be willing to talk to the
board of directors about inviting the living wage campaign leaders to a
meeting. However, this agency did publish an extensive report on self-
sufficiency wages, providing strong evidence for higher wages in the
community. Another agency (in this same campaign) when approached
about endorsement had expressed an interest in meeting with coalition
members, stating they might consider endorsement in due time. The
agency's professional social work director indicated "the agency was less
apt to support controversial issues such as prochoice but felt this living
wage issue may not fall into that same category." Both agencies asked the
coalition to keep them updated on the progress of the campaign and said
they would be glad to help in other ways such as spreading the word about
campaigns. However, neither offered an endorsement nor sought further
conversations concerning endorsements. Perhaps the coalition needed to
spend more time trying to convince these agencies to endorse the movement, or as one local activist stated, "I think getting one advocacy agency
on board would have encouraged other agencies to follow suit." However,
the coalition chose to spend its efforts getting larger numbers (versus
kinds) of agencies especially prior to the first organized event of the campaign, focusing on grassroots agencies along with other unions and
churches.

SPECULATIONS ON THE LACK OF SUPPORT
FOR LIVING WAGE CAMPAIGNS

Campaign organizers speculated on reasons why traditional social service agencies did not readily endorse living wage campaigns. For example,
one organizer who had social work training said that the social work graduate programs in her city were all "highly clinical" and thus less inclined

to become involved in policy advocacy work. However, she stated that the living wage policy issue might be one of the best and easiest polices for us to get involved in:

> I want to make something very clear first of all: the living wage policy fight is but a subset of any kind of public policy and advocacy work and social work doesn't get involved in this work in general [however] they may be more likely to participate in a living wage thing [compared to other policy work] because often it is the human service county or city worker who are low paid workers.

She added that an administrative or community organizing track is needed in social work schools in her state.

> Don't get me wrong, lots of people who go into social work do want to make a better world but to their credit they don't get support to do so; there is no atmosphere in the schools of social work to promote it.

Then she put the idea into a larger context in the United States in general, stating people don't get involved [in political movements]. She advocated for an international perspective in social work courses to remedy this lack of political involvement.

She later expressed disillusionment about the possibility of getting social work agencies involved in living wage campaigns. "Social work is a profession that keeps a lid on discontent by giving folks just enough, basically doing the job of the government. We are the surrogates for the government." She felt the "professionalization of helpers" has robbed people of their natural process to support policies that would help clients and workers in their agencies, for that matter. A respondent on a welfare Listserve echoed a similar theme: "I believe that in the world of social services, they are stuck in their own rules and regulations and cannot be of help."

Others felt social service agencies were just suffering from lack of funds due to state and federal cutbacks and so could not afford to alienate any local funders. One respondent faulted labor unions for ignoring the working poor until recently, which tended to alienate all social service agencies. Others saw the social service agencies as resistant to labor organizing. Either way, it resulted in a rift between unions and social service agencies that may be playing out in the living wage movement.

In the researcher's experience of working in a living wage coalition, no social service agency workers specifically talked about losing funds if they supported living wage movements until the National Network for Women's Employment Women Work conference. A social service employee at the conference workshop expressed this concern. She said she felt restricted from discussing whether the agency should support a living wage movement because it would be seen as political organizing and that would threaten funding, particularly from the federal level. Another conference participate cited the Hatch Act as a policy that kept the agency from supporting political issues such as a living wage. However, we talked about how that may well be a misinterpretation of the Hatch Act (U.S. Office of Special Council, n.d.) and similar policies. Conference participants were uncertain as to how much of their time could be spent committed to lobbying for changes in policy to avoid threatening their agency's nonprofit status or funding.

The threat of a loss of funds is especially real today in social service agencies. However, all respondents suggested that instead of giving up and just accepting this as something social service agencies cannot do, organizers need to encourage social service agencies to participate by offering solutions. Suggestions included making sure a living wage policy exempts nonprofit organizations from the provisions of the ordinance; finding a way to end the conflict between unions and social service agencies; and teaching master-level social workers the importance of policy advocacy and community organizing. Specifically only one of 25 students in the graduate social work policy advocacy course taught by one of the authors while conducting this research knew about ACORN and none of them knew about the living wage movement. Several of these concentration-year students expressed an interest in the living wage movement for their policy advocacy project. Two students choose to help organize the poverty forum as their policy advocacy project. One of these students, the one who knew about ACORN, said the class provided her with the "incentive to get involved with the organization." She became one of five speakers at the first poverty wage forum to support a living wage.

SUMMARY AND RECOMMENDATIONS

Upon examination of social work and traditional social service agencies' involvement in living wage campaigns, findings indicate that with noted exceptions, this involvement is minimal at best. Social workers and the agencies in which they work appear to be unwilling or unable to take a stand for various reasons, some realistic, some not. With the advent of devolution, social service agencies must increasingly seek and rely on local funding sources. Taking stances on policies such as living wages may threaten this funding. Thus, solutions to increasing willingness to publicly endorse campaigns such as the living wage cause risks to individual agencies but provide benefits for empowering poor and working-class "clients" and for the social work profession itself. Social workers and social service agencies may be willing but uncertain how to proceed in taking some risks and actively support living wage campaigns. Taking this risk is necessary as the NASW Code of Ethics and the International Federation of Social Workers (IFSW) specifically state that social workers must work for social justice. The IFSW goes further as can be seen in Principal 4.2 titled Social Justice:

> Challenging unjust policies and practices – Social workers have a duty to bring to the attention of their employers, policymakers, politicians and the general public situations where resources are inadequate or where distribution of resources, policies and practices are oppressive, unfair or harmful. (IFSW, 2006)

In addition, Council of Social Work Education (CSWE) Educational Policy and Accreditation Standards include a call for using policy practice skills to influence and advocate for policy consistent with social work values (CSWE, 2003, p. 35).

For the social work profession and social service agencies to have an opportunity to return to our progressive roots, we must call one another to task on strategic ways to support such movements. We must work with other agencies, grassroots organizations, and community organizers of various social policy issues to plan our support.

Established community organizing approaches and models have not been effectively understood and utilized by social service agencies, nor adapted to social service agencies' situations and related needs in the postwelfare reform climate. In an effort to find a model to promote community organizing that might be useful for direct social service agencies, the authors suggest using familiar direct practice approaches for involving traditional social service agencies in community organizing and social action movements. Since social service agencies focus on helping the individual and family, a behavior change model traditionally used for such work might also be used to help the agency move toward community organizing work. As illustrated in Table 1, use of a Stages of Change Model could offer individual social workers (and others) within organizations the

TABLE 1. Stages of change model with added strategy for social action*

Stage	Definition	Potential Change Strategies	New Approach for Agency Workers & Outside Organizers
1. Precontemplation	Has no intention of taking action within the next six months	Increase awareness of need for change; personalize information on risks and benefits	Learn how social action issue impacts both clients and employees of agency. Find supporters of social action issue within the agency and identify other supporters outside of the agency. Make presentations, distribute handouts
2. Contemplation	Intends to take action in the next six months	Motivate; encourage to make specific plans	Identify key stakeholders within agency and develop linkages with social action organizers from the community for planning purposes
3. Preparation	Intends to take action within the next thirty days and has taken some behavioral steps in this direction	Assist in developing concrete action plans and setting gradual goals	Assist agency with plan of action, to include: 1) active participation, 2) remaining neutral (with or without client involvement), and 3) inactive participation
4. Action	Has changed behavior for less than six months	Assist with feedback, problem solving, social support, and reinforcement	Social action plan implemented with a network consisting of agency, other social service agencies, and outside community organize
5. Maintenance	Has change behavior for more than six months	Assist in coping, reminders, finding alternatives, and avoiding slips/relapses (as applies)	Ongoing education and support. Information and support regarding potential conflicts and accomplishments

*Initial Model from National Cancer Institute (2005). Expanded via addition of fourth column.
SOURCE: National Cancer Institute. (2005). Theory at a glance, a guide for health promotion, 2nd. Ed. Bethesda, MD: National Institutes of Health. Downloanded July 7, 2007 from http://www.cancer.gov/theory.pdf.

tools needed to affect change from within (National Cancer Institute. 2005). In addition, community organizers would benefit from "starting where the client is" by approaching organizations on familiar, more clinical, terms – a strategy that may be more applicable and effective in today's professional climate.

This "stages of change" model uses an ecological perspective to guide interventions for change on multiple levels through the use of cognitive-behavioral and environmental components. The findings from this case study indicate potential exists for participation of social service agencies in community organizing efforts because, among other things, individual social workers within some agencies are already interested or active in a particular community organizing effort. In a few cities, these agencies have become active in community organizing activities already. However, successful involvement of these agencies most likely requires unique and gradual efforts and strategies from within and from without— from other social service agencies, grassroots organizations, and the community organizers from a particular campaign. The model is enhanced from its original form to include a fourth column that offers basic suggestions of strategies based on the findings from this study. Further research is needed to implement this strategy with one or more social service agencies, evaluating its effectiveness in securing the involvement of direct service agencies with community organizing efforts.

REFERENCES

Abramovitz, M. (1998). Social work and social reform: An arena of struggle. *Social Work, 43*(6), 512–526.

ACORN (2005). *ACORN History: Roots of a social justice movement (1970–1975)*. Retrieved on October 18, 2005, from www.acorn.org/index.php?id=2757.

Amott, T. L. (1990). Black women and AFDC. In L. Gordon (Ed.), *Women, the State and Welfare* (pp. 280–298). Madison, WI: University of Wisconsin.

Brooks, F. (2005). Resolving the dilemma between organizing and services: Los Angeles ACORN's welfare advocacy. *Social Work, 50*(3), 262–269.

Council on Social Work Education, (CSWE) Commission on Accreditation (2003). *Handbook of Accreditation Standards and Procedures*,(5th ed.). Alexandria, VA: CSWE.

Hyde, C. (1996). A feminist response to Rothman's "The interweaving of community intervention approaches." *Journal of Community Practice, 3*(3/4), 127–145.

International Federation of Social Workers (IFSW) (n.d.). *Ethics in social work: Statement of principles*, Retrieved on June 8, 2006, from http://www.ifsw.org/en/p38000015.html.

Jansson, B. S. (2003). *Becoming an effective policy advocate: From policy practice to social justice* (4th ed.). Pacific Grove, CA: Brooks/Cole.

Karger, H. J., & Stoesz, D. (2006). *American social welfare policy: A pluralist approach* (5th ed.). Boston: Allyn & Bacon.

Kreuger, L. W., & Neuman, W. L. (2006). Chapter 13: Qualitative data collection and analysis. In *Social work research methods: Qualitative and quantitative applications* (pp. 365–392). Boston: Pearson Education.

Living wage campaign. (2006). (ACORN).Retrieved on June 8, 2006, from http:// www.livingwagecampaign.org/index.php?id=1958.

Living wage resource center. (2005) (ACORN) Retrieved on July 7, 2005, from http:// www.livingwagecampaign.org/index.php?id=2071.

Luce, S. (2004). *Fighting for a living wage.* Ithaca: Cornell University.

U.S. Office of Special Council (OSC) (n.d.) *Political activity (Hatch Act).* Retrieved on June 11, 2006, from http://www.osc.gov/hatchact.htm.

National Cancer Institute. (2005). *Theory at a glance, a guide for health promotion,* 2nd. ed. Bethesda, MD: National Institutes of Health.

Rothman, J. (1996). The interweaving of community intervention approaches. *Journal of Community Practice, 3*(3/4), 69–99.

Specht, H., & Courtney, M. E. (1994). *Unfaithful angels: How social work has abandoned its mission.* New York: Free Press.

Tandon, R. (1981). Participatory research in the empowerment of people, *Convergence,14* (*3*), 20–29.

Technology-Based Approaches
to Social Work and Social Justice

Judith M. Dunlop
Graham Fawcett

The development of social software or free software has created exciting opportunities for social work practitioners and nonprofit organizations (NPOs) to level the playing field between "haves" and "have nots" in the information age. The creation of social software (free software) represents a move toward equality as nonprofit organizations, previously shut out of the information technology arena, are no longer excluded. Although information technology (IT) can be used as a tool to extend traditional advocacy methods, it is too expensive for most nonprofit organizations. With the advance of social software or "free software", nonprofit organizations can play a major role in the development of electronic advocacy by sharing their knowledge and expertise with diverse stakeholders across multiple technological routes.

Thus, the utilization of social software has quickened the pace of change in nonprofit organizations and broadened the strategies that help to create effective advocacy. Electronic advocacy has been defined as a social work practice method that uses high technology to influence policy decision making (Fitzgerald & McNutt, 1999; Hick & McNutt, 2002). Social software alone does not promote electronic advocacy. In the twenty-first century, the route to electronic advocacy is a partnership between IT-skilled social workers and service providers who strive to become technologically competent. Of concern then is whether social workers can provide this expertise and assist organizations to: (1) enter the information age, (2) use technology-based approaches to help disadvantaged populations, and (3) implement electronic advocacy practice to promote social justice in local communities. Considerable commitment is needed to change the social work curriculum so that social work practitioners can use technology-based approaches and assist NPOs to enter the information age and implement electronic advocacy practice.

This paper begins with historical perspectives on social work advocacy and examines both traditional and electronic advocacy practice. Next, it explores various types of social software or free software that would be useful to nonprofit organizations. Finally, it theorizes about the application of social software to social work advocacy practice in this century.

HISTORICAL PERSPECTIVES: SOCIAL WORK ADVOCACY

A comprehensive look at social work advocacy practice throughout history is beyond the scope of this paper; however, a brief review illuminates its importance to social work practice. Social work's history of advocacy for social change spans more than 100 years (1869–1999) (Rothman, 1995; Weil & Gamble, 1995). In the late 1800s and early 1900s, the Charity Organization Society and the Settlement House Movement were actively involved in their own versions of advocating for social justice. Workers associated with the Charity Organization Society directed their advocacy efforts to individuals and families who were unemployed and poor. In contrast, the Settlement House Movement advocated for marginalized populations at the neighborhood level. During the 1920s and 1930s, social work as a profession became preoccupied with psychiatric casework and Settlement House workers gradually turned their attention away from social action strategies to educational and recreational programs (Trattner, 1999). In the 1940s and 1950s, focus shifted back toward community organization and the 1950s paved the way for the development of a model of social action based on labor and neighborhood organizing (Alinsky, 1971).

In the 1960s and 1970s, the development of advocacy planning advanced social action in community organization practice (Rothman, 1967; Alinsky, 1971; Lauffer,1978). The social and political changes in the 1960s encouraged the development of radical or structural models of practice that challenged the government's top-down policymaking.

During the 1980s, community organization offered advocacy groups an opportunity to organize collectively against the oppressive structures of the state (Friedmann, 1987; Mayo, 1984; Panet-Raymond, 1989). In the 1990s, as interorganizational collaboration became more prevalent as an instrument of public policy, new conceptualizations of advocacy were developed based on community planning with stakeholder constituencies of community leaders and human service providers (Rothman, 1995; Dominelli, 1990; Popple, 1996; Weil & Gamble, 1995). For some practitioners, there has been a shift in the twenty-first century to electronic advocacy practice. Although some overlap occurs between the two methods, traditional and electronic, more exploration is needed to connect these approaches.

ADVOCACY AND SOCIAL WORK PRACTICE

Traditional models of advocacy practice in social work reflect a commitment to social activism. Social activism may be defined differentially and interchangeably as (1) community organizing, (2) community development, (3) community participation, (4) policy practice, and (5) social action. Typically, traditional advocacy practice includes diverse strategies such as demonstrations, boycotts, and symbolic acts such as mock elections and street theater, lobbying, grassroots action and political action committees (Haskett, 2002; Jansson, 2005). Traditional advocacy includes both *case advocacy* (advocating for services for an individual client or group of clients) and *cause advocacy* (social action strategies to effect policy and legislative change) (Hick & McNutt, 2002; Jansson, 2005). Advocacy practice includes the following social work skills:

1. getting issues on the public agenda;
2. social marketing;
3. policy-related research to influence decision-makers;
4. preparation of briefs and proposals; and
5. reforming internal program operations.

Advocacy for social justice has been the focus of social work researchers, practitioners and educators over the past few years. Scholars have identified clearly how social workers can approach advocacy in a systematic way that integrates advocacy practice into generalist practice (Ezell, 2001; Hoefer, 2006; Schneider & Lester, 2000). However, despite this recognition of the need for social workers to acquire traditional advocacy skills, there has been some resistance to the concept of electronic advocacy as an emerging practice modality. This paper challenges this resistance to using technological approaches to advocacy practice and suggests that technology will lead the way for social workers in the future to create virtual communities and strong social justice communities both local and global.

Recently, scholars have questioned how social work can continue to carry out advocacy strategies using traditional models (McNutt, 2006; McNutt & Hick, 2002). Most agree that the question is not *whether* electronic advocacy is needed but *how* students will learn how to use technology-based approaches (Frey & Faul, 2005).

ELECTRONIC ADVOCACY AS AN EMERGENT FORM OF PRACTICE

Recognizing the importance of technology-based approaches does not imply that social workers will discontinue their traditional advocacy practice. It does suggest, however, that most situations social workers will face in the future will require new knowledge and technological skills such as using social software to increase the electronic advocacy capabilities of nonprofit organizations. New technology has created the need for social workers to learn how to organize virtual communities, carry out electronic policy advocacy, use geographical information systems and other planning software, and provide leadership in the development of competencies in using the internet as a tool for social justice.

The potential of electronic advocacy in social work is becoming well known. Although it has not replaced traditional advocacy, growing acceptance indicates that electronic advocacy is a powerful tool for social change. Despite these promising developments, some resistance to e-advocacy remains among social work educators and practitioners (Dunlop, 2006; McNutt, 2006). Social workers confront unique problems when attempting either to make the shift from traditional to electronic advocacy or to integrate both these approaches. These problems include (1) the changing nature of e-advocacy, and (2) the lack of IT expertise needed to mix these two advocacy methods (McNutt, 2006).

Information technology is an emerging tool for producing social change at local, state, national, and international levels. Social workers must understand that a technology-based approach such as using social software or "free software" shifts them from their traditional advocacy paradigm. In spite of this, both methods offer strategies that are key tools for promoting social justice.

INFORMATION TECHNOLOGY AND SOCIAL WORK EDUCATION

Changes in the information society have affected the way social workers practice. Consequently, social work educators must ensure that students learn new technology-based approaches to practice. This can happen only if social work educators themselves acquire the necessary knowledge and skills to support students as electronic advocates.

The terms "social software" and "free software" share some overlap, but emphasize different aspects of availability and freedom of use. Social software encompasses an Internet-enabled software that allows and encourages users to interact, collaborate, organize and share resources. It can include software owned by commercial interests as well as noncommercial offerings, but generally all social software programs are free for use. Free software can be examined, modified, distributed, and used without restriction. Free software has no monetary cost, but more important, it is free in the sense of freedom of use. Free software has different connotations in different technical communities; a popular and socially progressive definition is expressed by the Free Software Foundation (FSF).

Using social software in electronic advocacy practice includes the following free IT applications:

- blogs
- free email
- electronic mailing lists
- news groups
- photo-journalism
- word processing
- database management
- graphics editing tools
- financial management
- mapping tools
- reference tools/research tools.

As an example, with mapping tools such as Google Maps, it is now possible for agencies and practitioners to find user-friendly technology to graphically represent the demographics, service needs, resources, duplications, and service gaps that characterize specific geographical locations. The use of Geographical Information Systems (GIS) mapping expands the avenues by which social work practitioners can design, implement, and evaluate programs (Hoefer, Hoefer, & Tobias, 1994). However, the provision of educational opportunities tailored to the needs of social work practitioners is necessary if the profession is to take full advantage of the potential of GIS.

Nonprofits deserve to have the most advanced and free technological applications. Social work students and practitioners need to develop their skills and integrate traditional and electronic advocacy practice. In doing so, they reduce the "digital divide" and help nonprofit organizations promote equality for disadvantaged populations. Using e-advocacy skills to promote social justice demands that students and educators overcome their resistance to technology-based methods. Increasingly, the barriers to using information technology are based on human resistance, not the limits of technology. Overcoming this resistance will ensure that social workers expand the possibilities of promoting social justice in the twenty-first century.

SOCIAL SOFTWARE AND SOCIAL WORK PRACTICE

Information technology is an emerging tool for producing social change at local, state, national, and international levels. Social software is an important ally in the struggle for social justice. Social software and free software have created new parameters for electronic advocacy in social work. This software, which is readily available to nonprofit organizations, supports group communications, database management, web-based home page development, discussion groups, and other Internet-based communications. Social software has the ability to democratize information technology and build virtual communities among stakeholders who have a stake in social change.

Using social software to build networks allows social workers as advocates to spread information quickly and to organize supporters for social action across diverse geographical locations and issues. Social work practitioners, if educated in technology-based approaches to advocacy practice, could bring much-needed IT services to nonprofit organizations. Building the capacity of social work students to apply technology to advocacy practice benefits the student, the organization, and the population it serves.

Building digital democracy through free software that is user-friendly and accessible moves electronic advocacy into the realm of the possible for nonprofits. This social software is readily available to organizations that may not be able to afford commercial products or their copyright licenses. The challenge is not simply to identify the sites where this software may be accessed or downloaded but for social work practitioners to become experts in the use of this software. Organizations will need consultation and support to become proficient and autonomous in its use. We must remember that it is not enough to provide free software. We must also provide technical support to encourage and empower organizations to become technologically perceptive.

Building on this argument for technology-based approaches, the following review of available social software or free software provides an overview of the number of programs that nonprofits could use to move into the information age. Using this free software would strengthen both their advocacy practice and organizational capacity. Summaries of the following social software programs are presented: (1) blogs, (2) free e-mail, (3) electronic mailing lists, (4) news groups, (5) photojournalism, (6) word processing and spreadsheets, (7) database management, (8) graphics editing tools, (9) financial management, (10) mapping tools, (11) reference tools, (12) research tools, and (13) social networking tools and (14) social bookmarking. This section structures the discussion of social software into the following dimensions for each type of software: name of the software, a brief description of its function and purpose, and the URL where it may be accessed.

Blogs

Blog (or weblog) is a general term encompassing a variety of websites, ranging from online personal diaries to independent journalism sites. Blogs provide an online soapbox (one-way channel) and interactive forum (multiway conversation) for any person or group with Internet access. Blog sites frequently offer a comment system, allowing "visitors" to publish their own unmoderated opinions in the context of the blog postings.

Blog sites can be set up free of charge, through a variety of blogging services. Popular free blogging services include Blogger (http://www.blogger.com/) and LiveJournal (http://www.livejournal.com/).

Free E-mail

Free e-mail services services are usually web-based, meaning that users visit their "inbox" using a web browser; the actual messages are stored elsewhere on a web server, rather than on the user's personal computer. This enables access to e-mail from any Internet-enabled computer. In return for the free service, free e-mail companies expose users to advertising while they are viewing their e-mail.

Well-known services include Hotmail (http://www.hotmail.com/), Yahoo! Mail (http://mail.hotmail.com/) and Google Mail (http://gmail.com/).

Electronic Mailing Lists

Electronic mailing list is a more generic term for Listserv, which is a trademark name. Although a relatively old technology by Internet standards, electronic mailing lists are still a popular form of communication. List-serv enables a member of a mailing-list to send a message to all list members without a moderator's intervention. List membership actions (such as subscribing to and unsubscribing from the list) are also automated.

Recently, there has been a blurring of the lines between electronic mailing lists and newsgroups; many modern discussion tools allow users to "visit" the discussion by e-mail, a web browser, or a newsreader.

Popular free discussion-group tools include Yahoo! Groups (http://groups.yahoo.com/) and Google Groups (http://groups.google.com/). Groups may also choose to use mailing list software (such as Listserv, Majordomo or Mailman) on their own Internet servers.

News Groups

Predating the World Wide Web, the Usenet news system has been a constant source of online discussion for the past twenty years. Usenet has hosted numerous public discussion groups on a vast range of topics. According to Google Groups (a site that offers a web-based archive of Usenet), there are currently more than 54,000 discrete Usenet newsgroups.

As with e-mail, Usenet has no website of its own; however, most Usenet users tend to use web-based Usenet interfaces, such as Google Groups or Gmane (http://gmane.org/). These web-based systems also allow users to create their own discussion groups on new topics without the complications that once were required to create and propagate a Usenet group.

Photo Journalism

Numerous sites allow users to post photographs online, but the most popular currently is Flickr (http://flickr.com/). These sites make it simple to share photographs and short narratives with friends and colleagues as well as with the anonymous public. An interesting new service is Tabblo (http://www.tabblo.com/), which allows users to create photo presentations or posters rather than just collecting photos into a set or "stream" like Flickr.

Word Processing and Spreadsheets

Although tools such as WordPerfect and Microsoft Word are still tremendously popular in the workplace, their free equivalents have been catching up in popularity and overall quality. The most popular free office suite (including word processing, spreadsheets, presentation software, and graphics editing) is OpenOffice.org (http://openoffice.org). It is no longer necessary for individuals and groups with few resources to pay license fees for (or, worse, acquire pirated copies of) expensive commercial packages to perform basic office tasks such as word processing.

An interesting new spin in the free word-processing market is GoogleDocs (http://docs.google.com/) formerly known as Writely (http://www.writely.com/). GoogleDocs is a free web-based word processor and spreadsheet that can be accessed from anywhere, and in which users can collaboratively edit a document at the same time.

Database Management

Free applications for managing data include user-friendly tools such as OpenOffice.org, which includes a database application similar to (though not as sophisticated as) Microsoft Access. Users can describe the "tables" in which to store their information, and can create reports and forms using simple graphical tools.

If data need to be shared among many users, or centralized for other purposes, numerous server-based database applications are available that tend to be less "user friendly" but are extremely powerful tools. Popular database management systems include MySQL (http://www.mysql.com/) and PostgreSQL (http://postgresql.org/).

Graphics Editing Tools

There are many free tools for editing graphics, including OpenOffice.org, Inkscape (http://www.inkscape.org/), and Xara Xtreme (http://www.xaraxtreme.org/). One of the best-known and feature-rich tools is GIMP, the GNU Image Manipulation Program (http://www.gimp.org/). Users interested in editing graphics with free software are encouraged to give many tools a try, since they each have very different approaches to graphics editing, and may not all be suitable for specific needs.

Financial Management

Currently, commercial financial management tools are still well ahead of their free-software counterparts. A few tools with some promise are usable now and should continue to grow in capabilities in the coming years. These include KMyMoney (http://kmymoney2.sourceforge.net/), a personal finance-management tool for the Linux operating system, and GnuCash (http://www.gnucash.org/), which is more geared toward small-business management and is available for Windows and Mac as well as Linux.

Mapping Tools

Google Maps (http://maps.google.com/) is by far the most popular and sophisticated online map service. Google Maps also provides a "map API"—a means by which web programmers can connect their own websites to Google's mapping service, leading to a wide range of interesting "mashup" sites that combine Google's maps with someone else's information. For example, ChicagoCrime.org (http://www.chicagocrime.org/) overlays information on crimes in the Chicago area over Google's mapping data.

Though free to use for individuals and free, with permission, for "mashups" such as ChicagoCrime.org, online mapping tools tend to come with licenses that prevent online maps from unrestricted use. For example, Google Maps forbids reprinting of maps for nonpersonal use.

Reference Tools

Google Scholar (http://scholar.google.com/), is a well-known example of an online referencing tool. However, there is debate about its usefulness among many professional librarians, suggesting that there may be flaws in the service. Online reference services are evolving rapidly and the reader is encouraged to discuss their merits with a professional librarian. An intriguing new library-related site is LibraryThing (http://www.librarything.com/) a site that advertises itself as the "world's largest book club" and offers extensive information on books, reviews, and a very intelligent book recommendation service for popular and academic works.

Research Tools

Wikipedia (wikipedia.org) is a collaboratively written and edited encyclopedia The Wikipedia Foundation also hosts Wiktionary (http://www.wiktionary.org/), a collaboratively-created dictionary.

Social Networking Software

Facebook and MySpace are social networking software. A user can set up a space within these systems and link to other's spaces that are owned by the user's friends, family, and colleagues. One can form networks with friends and family but indirectly, one also forms extended networks of friends of friends and friends of family. While these sites have been used more for interpersonal networking, it is possible for activist groups to use social networking sites to spread a message beyond the converted few to their friends, family, and friends of friends.

Social Bookmarking Services

Unalog (http://www.unalog.com/) or Del.icio.us (http://del.icio.us/), allow users to share their web-browser bookmarks with others, and sometimes add comments on one another's bookmark lists. Unalog is not only social software but is free to download and run on an organization's private servers.

OTHER ELECTRONIC ADVOCACY DEVELOPMENTS

Two more recent technology developments for social justice advocacy merit brief mention in this final section. YouTube is a useful channel for spreading messages. Users are accustomed to sharing interesting YouTube links and assisting in spreading messages of social justice and social action. This has proven to be an effective strategy for environmental activists as they are able to send dramatic and emotive videos of polar bears on shrinking icebergs and baby seals being clubbed by hunters. More recently, political candidates have used YouTube to get their message across to large numbers of voters in the United States. Michael Moore has used YouTube videos to promote racial justice in the United States through his campaign to supply African Americans with Day-Glo wallets that are easily recognizable as nonthreatening (that is, they are not weapons) by police in the United States.

The second recent development is the use of technology to organize "Smart Mobs" to promote human action for social justice. Using high-speed communications such as cell phones and text messaging, social groups are able to organize virtual communities at a greater speed than ever before. "Smart Mobs" as socially-motivated, virtually-organized "mobs" are able to respond to local conditions in an organized and highly responsive manner, thus promoting participatory democracy and rapid advocacy strategies at local levels.

This brief review of what is available as free software can alert practitioners to think about how these resources could be used to support non-profit organizations. This raises the question of why we still have a "digital divide" (Steyaert, 2002). As early as 1996, questions were being asked about how to prevent a division between the technological "haves" and "have nots". Research has shown that when small local organizations are deprived of information technology tools, they become increasingly less effective compared with their better-resourced counterparts (Milio, 1996). Social software can widen the vision of nonprofits and provide a pathway to the use of technology-based approaches. In this paper, we argue that social workers can demonstrate how social software can be used in electronic advocacy. Other scholars, although not addressing the issue of free software directly, have identified technology-based approaches such as cyberadvocacy as an emerging specialty in social work macro practice (McNutt & Hick, 2002.

CONCLUDING REMARKS

The digital divide is not just about access to information technology. A gap in knowledge exists among nonprofit organizations regarding how to use technology-based approaches to respond to social problems. In this century, social workers must capitalize on technological change and overcome their resistance to learning new information technology skills, changing from traditional to electronic advocacy practice, and integrating traditional and electronic advocacy practice.

Social work's traditional models of advocacy need to be re-engineered to meet the challenges to social justice that result from an increasingly divided global economy. There is a need for technologically competent social workers to organize virtual communities, carry out electronic policy advocacy, and provide leadership in the development of electronic advocacy practice.

The emergence of social software is an innovation that marries the seemingly disparate worlds of social work and information technology. Nonetheless, in the compressed world created by technology, professions such as medicine, law, social work, nursing, and education are linked with IT specialists. Technology specialists whose democratic principles echo social work values have developed social software or "free software." More important, both human and technological elements must work together to promote social change (McNutt & Hick, 2002). Collaboration between these IT specialists and social workers creates a synergy that produces innovative practices that can change the worlds of technology "have nots."

This discussion has focused on how social work students, educators, and practitioners can apply technology-based approaches to their work with disadvantaged populations. Resistance to learning new technology skills has been identified as a future problem. However, emerging literature suggests social work students will receive more IT instruction and that cyberadvocacy practice will be the focus of curriculum development in the near future (Hick & McNutt, 2002). This paper has attempted to reinforce technology-based approaches by exploring the democratic promise of social software and its application to social work advocacy practice.

REFERENCES

Alinsky, S. (1971). *Rules for radicals.* New York: Random House.

Dominelli, L. (1990). *Women and community action.* Birmingham: Venture Press.

Dunlop, J. M. (2006). Onward and upward: A journey to somewhere. In J. M. Dunlop & M. J. Holosko (Eds.) *Journal of evidence-based social work, 3*(3/4), 221–231.

Ezell, M. (2001). *Advocacy in human services.* Belmont, CA: Brooks/Cole Thomas Learning.

FitzGerald, E., & McNutt, J. G. (1999). Electronic advocacy in policy practice: A framework for teaching technologically based practice. *Journal of Social Work Education, 35*(3), 331–341.

Frey, A. J., & Faul, A. C. (2005). The transition from traditional teaching to web-assisted technology. In R. L. Beaulaurier & M. Haffey (Eds.), *Technology in social work education and curriculum: The high-tech, high-touch social work educator* (pp. 91–101). Binghamton, NY: The Haworth Social Work Practice Press

Friedmann, J. (1987). *Planning in the public domain: From knowledge to action.* Princeton, NJ: Princeton University Press.

Haskett, G. (2002). Teledemocracy: Reinventing governance for social welfare. In S. Hick & J. McNutt (Eds.), *Advocacy, activism and the internet. Community organization and social policy* (pp. 173–182). Chicago, IL: Lyceum Press

Hick, S., & McNutt, J. (Eds.). (2002). *Advocacy and activism on the Internet: Community organization and social policy.* Chicago, IL: Lyceum Press.

Hoefer, R. (2006*). Advocacy practice for social justice.* Chicago: Lyceum Books.

Hoefer, R., Hoefer, R. M. & Tobias, R. (1994). Geographic information systems and social service administration. *Journal of Community Practice, 1*(3), 113–128.

Jansson, B. S. (2005). *Becoming an effective policy advocate: From policy practice to social justice.* Belmont, CA: Brooks-Cole.

Lauffer, A. (1978). The practice of social planning. In N. Gilbert & H. Specht (Eds.), *Handbook of the social services* (pp. 588–597). Englewood Cliffs, NJ: PrenticeHall.

Mayo, M. (1984). Partnerships for regeneration and community development. *Critical Social Policy, 17*(3), 3–26.

McNutt, J., & Hick, S. (2002). Cyberadvocacy as social work practice: The continuing challenge to reinvent the profession. In S. Hick and J. McNutt (Eds.), *Advocacy and activism on the internet* (pp. 223–229). Chicago: Lyceum Press

McNutt, J. (2006). Building evidence-based advocacy in cyberspace: A social work imperative for the new millennium. *Journal of Evidence-based social work, 3*(3/4), 91–102.

Milio, N. (1996). *Engines of empowerment. Using information technology to create healthy communities and challenge public policy.* Chicago: Health Administration Press.

Panet-Raymond, J. (1989). The future of community groups in Quebec: The difficult balance between autonomy and partnership with the state. *Canadian Social Work Review, 6*(1), 127–135.

Popple, K. (1996). Community work: British models. *Journal of Community Practice, 3*(3/4), 147–180.

Rothman, J. (1967). An analysis of goals and roles in community organization practice. *Social Work, 9*(2), 59–67.

Rothman, J. (1995). The interweaving of community intervention approaches. *Journal of Community Practice, 3*(3/4), 69–100.

Schneider, R. L., & Lester, L. (2000). *Social work advocacy: A new framework for action.* Belmont, CA: Wadsworth Publishing.

Steyaert, J. (2002). Inequality and the digital divide: Myths and realities. In S. Hick & J. McNutt (Eds.), *Advocacy and activism on the internet* (pp. 199–212). Chicago: Lyceum Press.

Trattner, W. I. (1999). *From poor law to welfare state. A history of social welfare in America* (6th ed). New York: The Free Press.

Weil, M., & Gamble, D. (1995). Community practice models. In R. Edwards (Ed.), *Encyclopedia of social work* (19th ed,) (pp. 577–594). Washington, DC: NASW Press.

The Supreme Court Shuffle: What It Means for Social Work

Sunny Harris Rome
Carolyn I. Polowy

BACKGROUND

Social work has a long tradition of advocacy and social action. From its earliest days, the social work profession was committed both to assisting individuals in need and to influencing environmental factors affecting human well-being. This commitment to social action was epitomized during the Progressive Era, when social workers made unprecedented strides in ameliorating harsh social conditions. Included in these movements were advocacy efforts focused on changing adverse policies. Successes included prison reform, the eight-hour workday, child labor laws, the establishment of kindergartens and orphanages, and improvements in hygiene and sanitation (Dolgoff & Feldstein, 2007).

In the past 40 years, social work has expanded and diversified its involvement in policy change. The National Association of Social Workers (NASW) focused its attention on legislative and political work by adding staff resources, by pursuing an annual legislative agenda that prioritizes national issues of concern to social workers, and by establishing a political action committee, PACE (Political Action for Candidate Election) (http://www.socialworkers.org).

The social work commitment to social action has also manifested itself in revisions to the NASW Code of Ethics. The most recent (1996, revised 1999) edition devotes an entire section to "Social Workers' Ethical Responsibilities to the Broader Society" including a specific subsection on "Social and Political Action":

Social workers should engage in social and political action that seeks to ensure that all people have equal access to the resources, employment, services, and opportunities they require to meet their basic human needs, and to develop fully. Social workers should be aware of the impact of the political arena on practice and should advocate for changes in policy and legislation to improve social conditions in order to meet basic human needs and promote social justice. (NASW, 1996, Standard 6.04).

Social work education likewise has intensified its commitment to teaching social policy and skills for policy change. Included in the most recent Educational Policy and Accreditation Standards (EPAS) is the requirement that programs provide curriculum content about:

- the role of policy in service delivery, social work practice, and attainment of individual and social well-being;
- the knowledge and skills to understand major policies that form the foundation of social welfare;
- the knowledge and skills to analyze organizational, local, state, national, and international issues on social welfare policy and social service delivery;
- the knowledge and skills to analyze and apply the results of policy research relevant to social service delivery; and

- the knowledge and skills to understand and demonstrate policy practice skills in regard to economic, political, and organizational systems, and use them to influence, formulate, and advocate for policy consistent with social work values. (Council on Social Work Education, 2003, p. 35)

During the 1990s, responsibility for many important social policy issues shifted from the federal government to the states in a process known as "devolution." In 1997, Influencing State Policy (ISP) was founded as a national forum for social workers dedicated to influencing legislative policy at the state level. ISP currently has faculty liaisons on 500 university campuses. It encourages schools of social work to organize Lobby Days in their states, offers training in legislative advocacy, awards prizes to students and mentoring faculty engaging in policy advocacy, and hosts a website that provides up-to-date information on state-level domestic policy issues.

Additional evidence of the profession's interest in policy practice includes The Policy Conference, a national gathering of social work faculty, students, and practitioners sponsored by the School of Social Work at Virginia Commonwealth University – and the biennial, regional Policy Practice Forum on Capitol Hill, sponsored by the Social Work Department at George Mason University.

TARGETING POLICY CHANGE

Not surprisingly, social work's attention to the policy process has focused almost exclusively on the legislative branch of government. After all, we think of the legislature's role as being *to make the laws*. The legislative branch is also the most amenable to influence: its members are elected, rather than appointed, and are therefore motivated to respond to constituents' concerns. Lobbying firms, organizations, and staff devote the majority of their resources to *legislative* advocacy, whether at the national, state, or local level.

It is important to remember, however, that all three branches of government play important roles in the policy-making process. Whereas the legislature's primary function is to make laws, it is the executive branch, through its administrative agencies, that promulgates regulations affecting the application and enforcement of the laws. Regulations can have important consequences for social workers and clients, because they translate the laws—which can be vague or inconsistent—into workable rules for implementation.

The judicial branch can also play a significant role in policy making. By interpreting statutory or constitutional law, the courts set the standards for legally acceptable individual and societal conduct. Because of the scope of its authority and its ability to apply federal constitutional law as the law of the land, the Supreme Court in particular exercises far-reaching influence on the policy landscape.

Each term, the Supreme Court issues decisions that impact social workers and their clients. In the past several years alone, the Court has issued important opinions on cases concerning special education, sex discrimination, capital punishment, immigration, Medicare and Medicaid, privacy rights, the right to die, gay rights, parental rights, hate crimes, domestic violence, welfare reform, gangs, mental health, disabilities, employment discrimination, terrorism, freedom of speech, affirmative action, rights of prisoners and criminal defendants, fair housing, legal services, sex offenders, cross burning, redistricting, reproductive rights, and family & medical leave (Legal Information Institute, 2006). Social work educators and professionals have made great strides in emphasizing the importance of legislative policy making, yet comparatively little attention has been paid to the huge impact of judicial policy making. Understanding the judiciary, especially the U.S. Supreme Court, is essential to an appreciation of the importance of policy to social work practice. Understanding how to influence judicial policymaking is essential to a full understanding of policy practice.

THE SUPREME COURT SHUFFLE

For more than a decade, until August 2005, the United States Supreme Court was comprised of the following nine members (year of appointment and appointing president are in parentheses): Chief Justice William Rehnquist (1972, Nixon; elevated 1986, Reagan), John Paul Stevens (1975, Ford), Sandra Day O'Connor (1981, Reagan), Antonin Scalia (1986, Reagan), Anthony Kennedy (1988, Reagan), David Souter (1990, G.H.W. Bush), Clarence Thomas (1999, G.H.W. Bush), Ruth Bader Ginsberg (1993, Clinton), and Steven Breyer (1994, Clinton).

Analysts considered the Court to be a conservative one, though the justices often were closely divided on controversial issues, as evidenced by the issuance of multiple concurring and/or dissenting opinions. These 5-4 decisions proved to be common, with Justice O'Connor often acting as the swing vote. She joined the more liberal justices on issues involving sexual harassment (*Davis v. Monroe Co. Board of Education,* 1999), campaign finance reform (*FEC v. Colorado Republican Federal Campaign Committee,* 2001), abortion (*Stenberg, v. Carhart,* 2000; *Hodgson v. Minnesota,* 1990; *Planned Parenthood of Southeastern Pennsylvania v. Casey,* 1992), prayer in schools (*Lee v. Weisman,* 1992), affirmative action in higher education (*Grutter v. Bollinger,* 2003), disability rights (*Tennessee v. Lane,* 2004), and capital punishment (*Atkins v. Virginia,* 2002). In other cases, however, she tipped the scales in favor of more conservative outcomes. Examples include voting rights (*Holder v. Hall,* 1994; *Shaw v. Hunt,* 1996), gay rights (*Boy Scouts of America v. Dale,* 2000), criminal sentencing (*Ewing v. California,* 2003), affirmative action in business contracts (*Adarand Constructors, Inc. v. Pena,* 1995), gender-motivated violence (*United States v. Morrison,* 2000), and states' rights (*United States v. Lopez,* 1995).

During the elections of 2000 and 2004, rumors abounded that Chief Justice Rehnquist and/or Justice O'Connor would soon be retiring. Activists on both sides emphasized the likelihood that the next president would have the opportunity, not seen since 1994, to make new appointments to the U.S. Supreme Court, potentially shifting its balance on important national concerns. The issue of Supreme Court appointments never gained much traction with the public. Yet the prognosticators proved to be correct.

Shortly after the 2004 election in which President George W. Bush won a second term, Chief Justice Rehnquist's health concerns began to interfere with his full participation on the Court. On July 1, 2005, amid rumors that Rehnquist would soon resign, Justice O'Connor announced her intention to retire as soon as a new Justice could take her seat (Baker, 2005, July 2). Conservatives pressed President Bush to appoint someone who would solidify the Court's leaning to the right, while liberals geared up for a fight. President Bush nominated a well-respected conservative, Judge John G. Roberts, to replace Justice O'Connor (Baker and VandeHei, 2005). When Chief Justice Rehnquist died in the midst of the confirmation process, President Bush withdrew Roberts from consideration for Justice O'Connor's seat and instead nominated him to assume the role of Chief Justice (Lane, 2005; Baker, 2005, September 6).

Next, President Bush nominated White House counsel Harriet Miers to replace Justice O'Connor. After several weeks during which both liberals and conservatives voiced their displeasure, she withdrew herself from consideration. President Bush then nominated Third Circuit Judge Samuel Alito, who was confirmed by the Senate after prolonged debate (Grunwald Becker, & Russakoff, 2005).

With Rehnquist and O'Connor (a conservative and an unpredictable swing voter) being replaced by Roberts and Alito (a conservative and an ultra-conservative), analysts predicted that the Court would shift notice-ably to the right. Many human service advocates and organizations, including NASW, were wary of what this might mean in terms of the Court's decisions affecting broad issues of social policy.

THE APPOINTMENT OF CHIEF JUSTICE ROBERTS

In the summer of 2005, NASW released a position statement on the potential appointment of John Roberts to the U.S. Supreme Court. The Association opposed his confirmation by the Senate on several grounds. First, NASW noted that appointing another white male to the Court would subjugate important diversity goals. Although women comprise slightly more than 50 percent of the U.S. population, the percentage of women on the Supreme Court (absent Justice O'Connor) would fall to only 11 percent. This was viewed as regressive political action, especially considering that women made up 32.3 percent of the available federal judges, 48 percent of law school students, and a substantial number of well-qualified practi-tioners.

Second, NASW raised concerns about Justice Roberts' record on reproductive choice. NASW's policy on the issue calls for "unimpeded access to family planning and reproductive health services, including abortion services" (NASW, 2003, p. 127). This is in keeping with the pro-fession's commitment to the value of client self-determination as articu-lated in the NASW Code of Ethics (1996). Justice Roberts' record reveals positions taken in prior cases that contradict the NASW policy statement. As noted in the NASW position statement (2005a, p. 3), Roberts argued in his brief before the U.S. Supreme Court in *Rust v. Sullivan* (1991) that *Roe v. Wade* "was wrongly decided and should be overruled." In *Bray v. Alexandria Women's Health Clinic* (1993), he contended that the efforts of antichoice protesters to interfere with women's access to an abortion clinic did not constitute gender discrimination.

Finally, concerns were articulated about civil rights issues. The NASW Code of Ethics requires social workers to prevent and eliminate discrimination, to expand choice and opportunity for all people, and to advocate changes in policy and legislation to improve social conditions and to promote social justice (NASW, 1996). NASW's Policy Statement on *Civil Liberties and Justice* (2003) specifies that NASW supports protecting the rights of criminal defendants, supports full implementation of existing civil rights laws, and supports the constitutional right to privacy (NASW, 2003). In several cases, Justice Roberts expressed positions that undermine support for civil rights protections. These included *Denton v. Hernandez* (1992), in which Roberts argued that the Court should limit the rights of prisoners or criminal defendants; *Burns v. United States* (1991), in which he argued that courts should be able to depart upward from sentencing ranges established by the Sentencing Guidelines without first notifying the parties involved; and two school desegregation cases (*Board of Education of Oklahoma Public Schools v. Dowell,* 1990; *Freeman v. Pitts,* 1992) in which he argued for lifting desegregation requirements.

THE APPOINTMENT OF JUSTICE ALITO

NASW also issued a Position Statement opposing the appointment of Samuel Alito on some of the same grounds, along with others (2005b). Diversity was again a consideration, given the retirement of Justice O'Connor and the fact that replacing her with a man would further reduce the representation of women on the highest Court.

Justice Alito's judicial record was far more revealing than Judge Roberts' had been, because of his tenure on the federal bench. In several important reproductive rights cases, Alito's judicial positions contradicted NASW policy statements. In *Planned Parenthood of Southeastern Pennsylvania v. Casey* (1991), Judge Alito wrote the sole dissenting opinion in support of a state requirement that women notify their husbands before obtaining an abortion. He was undeterred by the fact that battered women might face abuse as a result of the spousal notification requirement, arguing that it would affect too few women to constitute an "undue burden." The case was later appealed to the U.S. Supreme Court, where a majority (that included Justice O'Connor) found the provision unconstitutional. Even as part of the majority in a subsequent late-term abortion case (*Planned Parenthood of Central New Jersey v. Farmer,* 2000), Alito argued that the case should have been decided on narrower grounds, again raising questions about his commitment to preserving a woman's constitutional right to an abortion.

In several aspects of civil rights law NASW concluded that Alito's judicial positions did not support social work values. The first pertains to the constitutionality of searches and seizures under the Fourth Amendment. In *Baker v. Monroe Township* (1995) and *Doe v. Groody* (2004), Alito took an expansive view of law enforcement's right to conduct a search, arguing that warrants need not identify, with specificity, the particular person or people to be searched in order to be valid.

In several criminal cases, Alito argued that the rights of criminal defendants and prisoners should be further limited. Examples include *Riley v. Taylor* (2001), in which he voted to deny habeas corpus relief to an inmate asserting that his trial had been tainted by race discrimination in jury selection; *Banks v. Beard* (2005), in which he argued that it was constitutional for the state corrections department to restrict high-risk inmates' access to nonlegal and nonreligious newspapers, magazines, and photographs; and *Rompilla v. Horn* (2004) in which he authored the majority opinion that the failure of defense counsel to obtain mitigating evidence pertaining to the defendant's mental condition did not constitute ineffective assistance of counsel. This was another case that was reversed on appeal by the U.S. Supreme Court, with Justice O'Connor joining the majority.

Another area of concern was the right of employees to pursue claims of race and sex discrimination. Examples included *Sheridan v. E.I. DuPont deNemours* (1996), in which Alito was the sole dissenter in a case concerning the threshold for hearing a sex discrimination claim; *Bray v. Marriott Hotels* (1997*),* in which his dissent regarding the sufficiency of the plaintiff's claim was roundly criticized by the majority; and *Nathanson v. Medical College of Pennsylvania* (1991), where he again argued that the right of an employee to bring a discrimination claim should be limited, prompting criticism from the majority.

Finally, NASW raised concerns about Alito's record on issues regarding separation of church and state. The NASW Policy Statement on *Civil Liberties and Justice* (2003), espouses strong support for the constitutional principle of separation of church and state, recognizing that religious belief "is a personal and private matter that should neither be constrained nor promoted by the government in any way" (p. 44). In *American Civil Liberties Union of New Jersey v. Schundler* (1999) and *American Civil Liberties Union of New Jersey v. Township of Wall* (2001), Alito successfully upheld the constitutionality of a city holiday display containing a crèche and a menorah because a few secular symbols and signs had been added and because the religious symbols had been donated to the town. In

Child Evangelism Fellowship of New Jersey, Inc. v. Stafford Township School District (2004), Alito concluded that it was not a violation of the Establishment Clause for religious organizations to distribute religious materials to elementary school students through teachers, bulletin boards, and hallway displays.

SUPREME COURT OPINIONS IN 2005–2006: THE TRANSITIONAL TERM

Despite the concerns of social workers and other advocates, Judge Roberts and Judge Alito were confirmed as the new Chief Justice and Justice, respectively, of the U.S. Supreme Court. Their first term, beginning in October 2005, was one of transition. Although a number of important cases were decided, not all involved the participation of both new members of the Court. These decisions nonetheless are important for social workers to understand. Cases of special significance to social work interests are summarized in the following text. When Roberts and/or Alito did participate, we comment on their role in the cases' outcome.

Arlington Central School District v. Murphy. This case concerns a provision in the Individuals with Disabilities Education Act (IDEA) that allows the court to award "reasonable attorneys' fees" to the prevailing party challenging an individual education program (IEP). In this case, parents of a child with dyslexia and other cognitive disabilities successfully claimed that the school district had failed to meet their child's needs as required by law. In conjunction with their suit, they sought payment for an educational expert and consultant whom they had hired to assist them in the proceedings. Both the district and circuit courts found that the term "attorneys' fees" includes "expert fees." In a 6-3 decision authored by Justice Alito (and joined by Chief Justice Roberts, among others), the U.S. Supreme Court reversed, finding that the IDEA statute would have to unambiguously specify the coverage of expert fees for such fees to be granted; since it fails to do so, the parents cannot collect. The dissenting opinions relied on the statute's legislative history and the law's intent in concluding that expert fees should be covered. The outcome is a disappointment for families seeking to hold their own in a legal proceeding that can be challenging without the assistance of experts, and prohibitively expensive with them.

Burlington Northern & Santa Fe Railway Co. v. White. This case concerns retaliation for complaints about sex discrimination. Sheila White was suspended from her job as a forklift operator after complaining that her boss had sexually harassed her. Shortly thereafter, she was transferred to other, less desirable, duties without any change in pay or benefits. The question was whether the company's actions were prohibited under the legal definition of "retaliation." The lower courts had applied a variety of different standards. In a unanimous opinion authored by Justice Breyer, the U.S. Supreme Court held that protection from retaliation extends to both employment-related andnonemployment-related behavior occurring both inside and outside the workplace; that it covers all employer actions that would have been materially adverse to the employee; and that a reassignment of duties can constitute retaliatory discrimination. Both Chief Justice Roberts and Justice Alito participated in consideration of this case, which was a "win" for supporters of civil rights.

Dixon v. United States. In this case, a woman bought seven guns for her boyfriend, a convicted felon. She herself had previously been indicted for participating in a check-cashing scheme, which made the firearm purchase illegal. Once arrested, she defended her criminal activity by claiming that she had no choice, fearing that her abusive boyfriend would cause her or her daughters serious bodily harm if she did not comply with his wishes. She was convicted and lost her appeal. The issue was whether the defendant, or the government, has the burden of proving that the crime was committed under duress. In a 7-2 decision authored by Justice Stevens (with both Chief Justice Roberts and Justice Alito joining in the majority), the U.S. Supreme Court held that the defendant bears the burden of proving duress by a preponderance of the evidence. This outcome may place additional stress on those rendered vulnerable by relationship violence and other forms of coercion.

Garcetti v. Ceballos. This case concerns the definition of protected speech under the First Amendment. A deputy district attorney (Ceballos), in the course of his professional duties, found fault with an affidavit police had used as the basis for obtaining a search warrant. He notified his supervisors by written memorandum and recommended that the case be dismissed, but they proceeded with the prosecution. At trial, Ceballos was called to testify for the defendants regarding the inaccuracies in the affidavit. Subsequently, Ceballos was reassigned to a new position, transferred to a different courthouse, and denied a promotion. After losing an employment grievance, he filed suit in the district court, claiming retaliation. The lower courts split on the issue of whether the allegations in the memorandum constituted speech protected by the First Amendment. In a

5-4 decision authored by Justice Kennedy (with Roberts and Alito joining the majority), the U.S. Supreme Court found that the speech is not constitutionally protected because it was made by a public employee in the course of performing his job. While this case circumscribes constitutional protections—leaving existing federal and state whistle-blowing laws in force—the outcome may nonetheless have the effect of discouraging employees from voicing views that differ from those of their supervisors.

Gonzales v. Oregon. In this case, the Attorney General of the United States issued an interpretive rule announcing that using controlled substances to assist in suicide would not be considered legitimate medical practice, and that prescribing controlled substances for this purpose is considered illegal under the Controlled Substances Act. The state of Oregon, a pharmacist, a doctor, and several terminally ill patients challenged the rule, claiming that the Oregon Death with Dignity Act exempts from liability those who prescribe or dispense lethal doses of drugs to assist in suicide. Both lower courts found the interpretive rule invalid. In a 6-3 opinion authored by Justice Kennedy (in which Roberts, Scalia, and Thomas dissented), the U.S. Supreme Court agreed, finding that it is outside the Attorney General's scope of authority to prohibit medical treatment and patient care that the state has specifically authorized. This decision is a "win" for proponents of the right to die. This case preceded Justice Alito's participation on the Court.

Hamdan v. Rumsfeld. Salim Hamdan, personal driver and bodyguard to Osama bin Laden, was captured by the Afghan militia forces, turned over to the U.S. military, and detained at the Guantanamo Bay Naval Base in Cuba. He was classified as an enemy combatant by a military commission convened in the aftermath of a 2003 presidential order authorizing such commissions. The U.S. Supreme Court accepted the case to consider whether these special commissions are properly authorized under Congress' Authorization to Use Military Force, the Uniform Code of Military Justice, or the inherent powers of the president. Also at issue was whether Hamdan is protected by the Geneva Convention. With Justices Alito, Thomas, and Scalia dissenting (and Chief Justice Roberts not participating in consideration of the case), the Court's majority found that President Bush overstepped his authority in constituting these special military commissions that fall outside existing law, and that the protections of the Geneva Convention do apply. The opinion sent a clear message that, regardless of how potentially dangerous the individual, the president must comply with the prevailing rule of law in subjecting him to trial and sentencing. This was one of a number of cases challenging the president's handling of the "war on terror" and examining the balance among the branches of government, and between national security and human rights.

Randall v. Sorrell. This case concerns a challenge to a Vermont law that strictly limits campaign contributions and expenditures. The claim underlying the challenge (by the ACLU, the Vermont Right to Life Committee, the Vermont Libertarian Party, and the Vermont Republican State Committee) is that the limits restrain freedom of speech and association under the First Amendment. The lower courts struck down some aspects of the bill and upheld others. The Supreme Court, in a 6-3 decision (with both Roberts and Alito joining the majority), found both the expenditure and contribution limits in this particular law to be excessive and therefore unconstitutional. The justices disagreed regarding the applicability—and continued viability—of *Buckley v. Valeo* (1976), the primary precedent in this area of the law. Both proponents and opponents of campaign finance reform considered the outcome in *Randall v. Sorrell* a victory, since the pivotal issue concerned the strictness of the limits, rather than the presence of limits in and of themselves.

Rumsfeld v. Forum for Academic & Institutional Rights, Inc. The group that brought this suit (FAIR) is a collection of law schools and law faculties that oppose discrimination, including discrimination based on sexual orientation. They took issue with the Solomon Amendment, which threatens the loss of federal funding for campuses that deny military recruiters access to their students. Citing the military's policies toward gays and lesbians, FAIR argued that conforming to the Solomon Amendment would require them to violate their own anti-discrimination policies, thus interfering with the first amendment rights to freedom of speech and association. The district court disagreed, but the circuit court found in FAIR's favor. In a unanimous decision authored by Chief Justice Roberts, the U.S. Supreme Court reversed, arguing that the Solomon Amendment's requirements (hosting military recruiters in the same way they host other recruiters) does not impinge on the law school's First Amendment rights. Justice Alito did not participate in the consideration of this case.

Scheidler v. National Organization for Women, Inc. This class action suit claimed that individuals and organizations opposing abortion were guilty of racketeering by virtue of conspiring to shut down abortion clinics through the use of violence and other coercive tactics. In a unanimous ruling authored by Justice Breyer, the U.S. Supreme Court disagreed. It applied a narrow reading of the statute, concluding that physical violence unrelated to robbery or extortion falls outside the purview of the racketeering law. This closes one legal avenue for abortion proponents seeking to stop interference with the right to reproductive choice. Justice Alito did not participate in the consideration of this case.

DISCUSSION

At the close of the 2005–2006 transitional term, it was still too soon to draw conclusions about the precise differences made by the new members of the Supreme Court. However, some general observations were possible. When Chief Justice Roberts joined the Court, his stated agenda was to minimize divisiveness and seek greater consensus (Legal Information Institute, 2006). The Court seemed to have begun to achieve this goal by emphasizing narrow rulings that leave larger, more controversial issues undecided. During the 2005–2006 session, nearly half of the Court's 72 decisions were unanimous, while less than one-fourth were decided by a single vote (Legal Information Institute, 1996). This is in sharp contrast to the record of the previous session, in which 5-4 decisions were commonplace.

As for predictions that the new Court would generate distinctly more conservative outcomes, the results are mixed. Some decisions were surprisingly supportive of liberal positions, whereas others reinforced recent conservative trends. The Court's decision in *Burlington v. White*, for example, represented an expansive view of the circumstances permitting a claim under Title VII of the Civil Rights Act of 1964 for retaliation in the face of employment discrimination.

The outcomes were less consistent in those cases regarding criminal procedure. Although Justice Alito authored a unanimous opinion supporting the right of criminal defendants to introduce evidence of third party guilt (*Holmes v. South Carolina*), other decisions (*Oregon v. Guzek; Washington v. Recuenco*) limited the rights of criminal defendants in the sentencing phase of a criminal trial.

The Court remained divided on issues concerning capital punishment as well. A challenge to the use of lethal injection (*Hill v. McDonough*) was decided on the narrowest possible grounds, affirming the right of death row inmates to challenge the procedure as a civil rights violation, but failing to reach the question of whether lethal injection itself is constitutional. In another case (*Kansas v. Marsh*), the majority of a divided

Court affirmed the applicability of the death penalty when mitigating and aggravating factors are equally balanced.

The Court's decisions on First Amendment issues also went in both directions. *Rumsfeld v. FAIR* and *Garcetti v. Ceballos* limited the right to free speech and freedom of association. By contrast, in *Gonzales v. O Centro Espirita Beneficente Uniao Do Vegetal,* the Court upheld the right of bona fide religious groups to import Schedule I substances for ritual use.

Although the Court's decisions in the 2005–2006 term reflected outcomes both consistent and inconsistent with social work values, it should be noted that both Chief Justice Roberts and Justice Alito—as predicted—voted overwhelmingly with the conservative block.

SUPREME COURT OPINONS IN 2006–2007: THE FIRST TRUE TEST

The Supreme Court recently completed its 2006–2007 term, the first term in which both Chief Justice Roberts and Justice Alito participated fully. Selected issues of interest to social work are profiled in the following. The roles of both new justices are highlighted.

Separation of Church and State

In *Hein v. Freedom of Religion Foundation* (decided June 25, 2007), a group of taxpayers opposed to government endorsement of religion challenged activities under the President Bush's Faith-Based and Community Initiatives program as violating the required constitutional separation of church and state. The Supreme Court, in a plurality opinion authored by Justice Alito (and joined by Chief Justice Roberts) held that ordinary taxpayers lacked the standing to bring an establishment clause claim in this case, in which Congress neither created nor funded the programs in question. The Court distinguished this case from an earlier one, *Flast v. Cohen,* which had granted taxpayers standing to challenge the use of federal funds for religious purposes. In a separate opinion, Justices Scalia and Thomas concluded that *Flast* should simply be overruled. The dissenting justices, in an opinion by Souter, wrote that the logic of the *Flast* case should be controlling. The plurality opinion here diminishes the rights of taxpayers to challenge certain perceived violations of the establishment clause, shielding the president's faith-based initiative from challenge and reinforcing the intermingling of government and religious affairs.

Criminal Justice

The Court considered two cases that concerned the jury's right to hear mitigating factors in death penalty cases, *Abdul Kabir v. Quarterman* and *Brewer v. Quarterman* (decided April 25, 2007). In 5-4 decisions, with Chief Justice Roberts and Justice Alito joining the dissent, the Court held that the judges in the lower court had erred in limiting the jury's consideration of potentially mitigating factors including childhood abandonment, abuse and neglect, mental illness, and chemical dependency. The case turned on whether the Eighth Amendment requires the jury to give "full effect" or only "some effect" to the defendant's mitigating evidence. The outcome bolsters the rights of criminal defendants in capital cases to have all mitigating evidence considered by the jury at sentencing.

Another death penalty case, *Panetti v. Quarterman* (decided June 28, 2007) concerns a murder defendant who was sentenced to death despite a history of mental illness. During the state and federal trials, he failed to claim that he was incompetent to be executed, but instead raised the claim only after the trail court set an execution date. In a 5-4 decision written by Justice Kennedy, the Supreme Court found the trial court to have erred in not providing the defendant with a hearing and an opportunity to provide expert psychiatric testimony. They also found the Circuit court to have applied too narrow a definition of incompetency. Although this defendant understood that the State wanted to execute him for murder, he suffered from delusions that led him to believe that the State actually wanted to execute him to keep him from preaching. The Supreme Court concluded that execution, under these circumstances, would serve no purpose since the defendant's understanding of the punishment was so divorced from reality. Consistent with their positions in the earlier two cases, Chief Justice Roberts and Justice Alito joined the dissenting opinion.

Free Speech

The Supreme Court reviewed issues affecting First Amendment free speech rights in two very different cases. In *Morse v. Frederick* (decided June 25, 2007), Chief Justice Roberts issued a 5-4 opinion upholding the actions of a high school principal in prohibiting a student from displaying a banner reading "Bong Hits 4 Jesus" at a school sponsored event. Roberts cited the banner's support of drug use, as well as its nonpolitical nature, in concluding that the expression at issue did not merit First Amendment protection. In a separate opinion, Justice Alito took pains to underscore that the he supported the restriction only insofar as the speech was advocating illegal drug use; he opposed any broader application that would restrict speech on social or political issues. The majority opinion here is significant because it erodes the protection of student free speech outlined in a 1969 landmark case (*Tinker v. Des Moines Independent Community School District*) where students wearing black armbands in protest of the Vietnam War were held to be engaged in protected speech. In that case, the Court famously opined that students do not leave their constitutional rights at the schoolhouse gate. In *Morse,* Justice Thomas argued that the *Tinker* rule protecting student free speech should be overruled entirely as contrary to the history of American education and to the goal of maintaining order in the schools. The dissenting justices argued that the banner was not in fact intended to promote drug use among students, but rather to attract the attention of the media.

In a very different First Amendment case, *Federal Election Commission v. Wisconsin Right to Life, Inc.* (decided June 25, 2007), the Court struck down a *provision* in the Bipartisan Campaign Reform Act of 2002 that prohibits advertisements, aired in the final weeks before a federal election, that name a particular candidate for office. The challenge was brought by a collection of organizations from across the political spectrum. The Court's analysis, authored by Chief Justice Roberts, turned on the distinction between "explicit advocacy" (communication that promotes a candidate's election or defeat) and "issue advocacy" (discussion of policy issues). In seeking to define what constitutes "explicit advocacy or its functional equivalent," the Court rejected tests that look to the speaker's intent or the effect on an election. Instead, it adopted an interpretation requiring an objective assessment of the communication's substance. Applying that test to the advertisements in question, the Court found them to be "issue advocacy" and therefore outside the bounds of speech that could be regulated. The Court's position in this case is contrary to its ruling in an earlier case (*McConnell v. Federal Election Commission*) that upheld the provision in question. In his dissent, Justice Souter (joined by Justices Stevens, Ginsburg, and Breyer) found the ads in question to be an example of using issue ads to advocate the election for defeat of a candidate. Souter emphasized the reasoning behind the Campaign Reform Act's prohibition: to reduce the influence wielded by well-financed corporations and unions on the electoral process. He stressed the importance of regulating publicity financed by special interests in order to reduce cynicism and restore public confidence in elections.

Immigration

In *Lopez v. Gonzales* (decided December 5, 2006), the Court considered a South Dakota case in which deportation proceedings were initiated against a legal permanent resident alien convicted of aiding and abetting another person's possession of cocaine—a felony under state law, but a misdemeanor under the federal Controlled Substances Act. In an 8-1 decision authored by Justice Souter (and joined by both Chief Justice Roberts and Justice Alito), the Court reversed the lower court holdings and ruled that, in order to trigger deportation by the Immigration & Naturalization Service, the crime must constitute a felony under the Controlled Substances Act. Given the pervasive controversy over immigration law and the current anti-immigrant sentiment in the country, this can be considered a generous outcome. It was based entirely, however, on a reading of the legislative language and did not involve any discourse on the immigration issue in general.

Reproductive Rights

A closely divided Supreme Court rejected challenges to the federal Partial-Birth Abortion Ban Act in *Gonzales v. Carhart* and *Gonzales v. Planned Parenthood* (decided April 18, 2007). This constitutes the first time the Court has upheld a federal ban on a specific abortion procedure. Leading the Court in its 5-4 decision was Justice Anthony Kennedy, who authored the majority opinion rejecting arguments that the law unconstitutionally imposes an undue burden on a woman's right to an abortion, that its language is too vague, and that it fails to provide an exception to protect the health of the mother. The new appointees to the Court, Justices Roberts and Alito, joined the majority supporting the abortion ban.

This decision was a major policy shift for the Court on reproductive rights and signals a not-unexpected chipping away at the constitutional right to an abortion.

School Desegregation & Affirmative Action

On June 28, 2007, the Supreme Court decided two cases challenging the constitutionality of race-conscious assignment of students to public schools: *Parents Involved in Community Schools v. Seattle School District No. 1* and *Meredith v. Jefferson County Board of Education*. In both instances, the Court struck down their voluntary desegregation plans.

In the Seattle district, the racial makeup of the school is one criterion for high school admission decisions if schools are oversubscribed. In

Jefferson County (Louisville, KY), a desegregation plan requires black student enrollment in elementary schools to be maintained at 15–50 percent. Complaints in both cases were brought by white students denied their first-choice schools, arguing that they were impermissibly discriminated against on the basis of race. Similar to other recent cases on affirmative action in education (*Grutter v. Bollinger* and *Gratz v. Bollinger*), these cases were decided on a thin margin. Here, Justice Kennedy—rather than former Justice O'Connor—cast the all-important swing vote. As expected, Chief Justice Roberts (joined by Justice Alito) demonstrated hostility toward affirmative action, taking issue with the application of "white" and "nonwhite" categorizations and concluding that the school systems could have used race neutral remedies to meet their educational goals. The Court distinguished these cases from *Grutter,* in which race was only one of a variety of criteria applied in making admissions decisions, and the institution at issue was a university rather than an elementary or high school.

In a separate concurring opinion, Justice Kennedy expressed his concern that the plurality had underestimated the importance of promoting diversity and avoiding racial isolation. Nonetheless, he found that the school districts had failed to demonstrate the need for race-based classifications to meet those goals. In a passionate dissent, Justice Breyer (joined by Justices Stevens, Souter, and Ginsburg) railed against the plurality's opinion as desecrating the promise of *Brown v. Board of Education*. He reasoned that school desegregation constitutes a compelling public interest, and that the Constitution permits local communities to implement even race-conscious plans such as these in order to achieve it. The decisions in *Seattle* and *Jefferson County* continue a line of cases that have trumpeted concerns about "reverse discrimination" and eviscerated the protections afforded by affirmative action.

Sex Discrimination

In a 5-4 decision (written by Justice Alito and joined by Chief Justice Roberts), the Court rejected a claim of sex discrimination under Title VII in the case of *Ledbetter v. Goodyear Tire & Rubber Co., Inc.* After retiring from employment with Goodyear, Lilly Ledbetter filed with the EEOC, claiming that her salary was substantially lower than the salaries of her male counterparts because of sex-based pay discrimination. Although the trial court granted her back pay and damages, the Circuit Court reversed. The U.S. Supreme Court rejected Ms. Ledbetter's claim as coming too late; under the statute, actions must be filed within 180 days of the discriminatory act. They ruled that, although the consequence of alleged discrimination (the pay disparity) fell within the designated time, the act itself (each individual pay decision) did not.

The dissent found the majority's interpretation impractical, arguing that pay disparities often occur in small increments and often are evident only over the long term. They further noted that employees often lack timely access to information about their co-workers' salaries and thus may be unable to make a timely filing after each pay decision. Women's groups (and NASW) considered the majority's decision to be a major setback in workplace rights. Both new justices supported Goodyear.

Special Education

In *Winkelman v. Parma City School District* (decided May 21, 2007), the Court considered whether parents of a child with a disability have the right, under the Individuals with Disabilities Act (IDEA), to appear in court without a lawyer. The majority of the U.S. Supreme Court (including Chief Justice Roberts and Justice Alito) held that they do. In this case, the parents of a six-year-old boy with autism, dissatisfied with the outcome of both the IEP process and a subsequent due process hearing, took their case to trial. The case was dismissed on appeal for lack of counsel. According to the Supreme Court, parents have independent rights under IDEA that are enforceable in federal court. Regardless of whether or not it is permissible for nonlawyer parents to represent their children's interests, they can represent their own—which include a free and appropriate education for their child. This removes a potential barrier for many parents and is therefore considered a positive outcome by the social work community.

CONCLUSION

The actions of the U.S. Supreme Court can have far-reaching consequences for policies affecting social work interests. Today, we are faced with a newly constituted Court that is less diverse than its predecessor is and shows signs of moving toward a more conservative position.

An analysis of the first two terms—one in which Chief Justice Roberts and Justice Alito participated only in some cases, and one in which they participated fully—show distinctly different trends. In the transitional (2005–2006) term, the Court often chose to rule on narrow grounds, avoiding a showdown on potentially controversial issues. This appears to have led to a more balanced set of outcomes than many feared. Some decisions—including those on free speech, special education, and abortion—reinforced conservative viewpoints. Others, however—including those concerning criminal law, sex discrimination, and campaign finance—were inconsistent or reflected more liberal positions.

In the most recent (2006–2007) term, however, the Court took on a series of highly charged social issues. The semblance of greater consensus that emerged from the previous term evolved into a pattern of 5-4 decisions with conservatives comprising the majority. Chief Justice Roberts and Justice Alito were part of the majority or the controlling plurality in many of these cases, contributing to the Court's incursion into important rights in areas including separation of church and state, student speech, campaign finance, abortion, sex discrimination, and affirmative action. Justice Kennedy often was the swing vote, joining the majority more often than any of his colleagues. In many cases, the Chief Justice's avowed respect for precedent led the Court to tamper with previous cases without actually overturning them.

At this juncture, the shift in the Court's makeup appears to have had its biggest impact in relation to reproductive rights and affirmative action. The implications of the *Gonzales v. Carhart* abortion decision are enormous. The 5-4 majority that previously protected abortion rights has become a 5-4 majority against them. There is reason to believe that, as the Court moves forward, the same may hold true with respect to other areas of women's rights. Similarly, the Court's dismantling of voluntary school desegregation efforts may herald an end to affirmative action.

The upcoming terms will tell us more. It is imperative that social workers monitor the outcomes and consider the implications of future cases, many of which will continue to address closely-held social work values. We should also increase our efforts to have an influence on judicial policy making: by voicing our support or opposition to judges being appointed to the lower courts, by voting in judicial elections, and by encouraging our advocacy organizations to submit "friend of the court" *(amicus)* briefs in Supreme Court cases of consequence. Such actions have the potential to make our investment in policy change more comprehensive and thus more successful.

REFERENCES

Abdul-Kabir v. Quarterman, 127 S. Ct. 1654 (2007).

Adarand Constructors, Inc. v. Pena, 515 U.S. 200 (1995).

American Civil Liberties Union of New Jersey v. Schundler, 168 F. 3d 72 (3d Cir. 1999).

American Civil Liberties Union of New Jersey v. Township of Wall, 247 F. 3d 258 (3d Cir. 2001).

Arlington Central School District v. Murphy, 126 S. Ct. 2455 (2006).

Atkins v. Virginia, 536 U.S. 304 (2002).

Baker v. Monroe Township, 50 F. 3d 1186 (3d Cir. 1995).

Baker, P. (2005, September 6). Bush nominates Roberts as Chief Justice: President seeks quick approval with another seat left to fill. *The Washington Post*, p. A1.

Baker, P. (2005, July 2). O'Connor to Leave High Court. *The Washington Post*, p. A1.

Baker, P., & VandeHei, J. (2005, July 20). Bush chooses Roberts for Court: Appeals Judge for D.C. has conservative credentials. *The Washington Post*, p. A1.

Banks v. Beard, 399 F. 3d 134 (3d Cir. 2005).

Board of Education v. Oklahoma Public Schools v. Dowell, 498 U.S. 237 (1990).

Boy Scouts of America v. Dale, 530 U.S. 640 (2000).

Bray v. Alexndria Women's Health Clinic, 506 U.S. 173 (1991).

Bray v. Marriott Hotels, 110 F. 3d 986 (3d Cir. 1997).

Brewer v. Quarterman, 127 S. Ct. 1706 (2007).

Brown v. Board of Education, 347 U.S. 483 (1954).

Buckley v. Valeo, 424 U.S. 1 (1976).

Burlington v. White, 126 S. Ct. 2405 (2006).

Burlington Northern & Santa Fe Railway Co. v. White, 126 S. Ct. 2405 (2006).

Burns v. United States, 501 U.S. 129 (1991).

Child Evangelism Fellowship of New Jersey, Inc. v. Stafford Township School District, 386 F. 3d 258 (514 3d Cir. 2004).

Council on Social Work Education (2003). *Handbook of accreditation standards and procedures* (5th ed.). Alexandria, VA: Author.

Davis v. Monroe Co. Board of Education, 526 U.S. 629 (1999).

Denton v. Hernandez, 504 U.S. 25 (1992).

Dixon v. United States, 126 S. Ct. 2437 (2006).

Doe v. Groody, 361 F. 3d 232 (3d Cir. 2004).

Dolgoff, R., & Feldstein, D. (2007). *Understanding social welfare: A search for social justice*. Boston: Allyn & Bacon.

Ewing v. California, 538 U.S. 11 (2003).

Federal Election Commission v. Colorado Republican Federal Campaign Committee, 531 U.S. 431 (2001).

Federal Election Commission v. Wisconsin Right to Life, 127 S. Ct. 2652 (2007).

Flast v. Cohen, 392 U.S. 83 (1968).

Freeman v. Pitt, 503 U.S. 467 (1992).

Garcetti v. Ceballos, 126 S. Ct. 1951 (2006).

Gonzales v. Carhart, 127 S. Ct. 1610 (2007).

Gonzales v. O Centro Espirita Beneficente Uniao Do Vegetal, 546 U.S. 418 (2006).

Gonzales v. Oregon, 546 U.S. 243 (2006).

Gonzales v. Planned Parenthood, 127 S. Ct. 1610 (2007).

Gratz v. Bollinger, 539 U.S. 244 (2003).

Grunwald, M., Becker, J., & Russakoff, D. (2005, November 1). Comparisons to Scalia, but also to Roberts. *The Washington Post*, p. A1.

Grutter v. Bollinger, 539 U.S. 306 (2003).

Hamdan v. Rumsfeld, 126 S. Ct. 2749 (2006).

Hein v. Freedom of Religion Foundation, 127 S. Ct. 1037 (2007).

Hill v. Donough, 547 U.S. 573 (2006).

Hodgson v. Minnesota, 497 U.S. 417 (1990).

Holder v. Hall, 512 U.S. 874 (1994).

Holmes v. South Carolina, 547 U.S. 319 (2006).

Kansas v. Marsh, 548 U.S. 163 (2006).

Lane, C. (2005, September 4). Chief Justice William H. Rehnquist dies. *The Washington Post*, p. A1.

Ledbetter v. Goodyear Tire & Rubber Co., Inc., 127 S. Ct. 2162 (2007).

Lee v. Weisman, 505 U.S. 577 (1992).

Legal Information Institute (2006). *Supreme Court collection.* Retrieved from http://www.law.cornell.edu/supct/06highlts.html.

Lopez v. Gonzales, 127 S. Ct. 2127 (2006).

McConnell v. Federal Election Commission, 540 U.S. 93 (2003).

Meredith v. Jefferson County Board of Education, Oral argument, Supreme Ct. Docket No. 05-915 (December 4, 2006). Transcript retrieved June 4, 2007, from *http://www.supremecourtus.gov/oral_arguments/argument_transcripts/05-915.pdf.*

Morse v. Frederick, 127 S. Ct. 2618 (2007).

Nathanson v. Medical College of Pennsylvania, 926 F. 2d 1368 (3d Cir. 1991).

National Association of Social Workers (1996). *Code of Ethics.* Washington, DC: Author.

National Association of Social Workers (2003). *Social work speaks* (6th ed.). Washington, DC: Author.

National Association of Social Workers (2005a). *Position statement of the National Association of Social Workers (NASW) regarding the confirmation of Judge John G. Roberts to the United States Supreme Court.* Available: http://www.socialworkers.org.

National Association of Social Workers (2005b). *Position statement of the National Association of Social Workers (NASW) regarding the confirmation of Judge Samuel A. Alito, Jr. to the United States Supreme Court.* Available: http://www.socialworkers.org.

Oregon v. Guzek, 546 U.S. 517 (2006).

Panetti v. Quartermain, 127 S. Ct. 1654 (2007).

Parents Involved in Community Schools v. Seattle School District No. 1, Oral arguments, Supreme Ct. Docket No. 05-908 (December 4, 2006). Transcript retrieved June 4, 2007, from *http://www.supremecourtus.gov/oral_arguments/argument_transcripts/05-908.pdf.*

Planned Parenthood of Central New Jersey v. Farmer, 220 F. 3d 127 (3d Cir. 2000).

Planned Parenthood v. Casey, 505 U.S. 833 (1992).

Randall v. Sorrell, 126 S. Ct. 2479 (2006).

Riley v. Taylor, 277 F. 3d 261 (3d Cir. 2001).

Roe v. Wade, 410 U.S. 113 (1973).

Rompilla v. Horn, 355 F. 3d 233 (3d Cir. 2004).

Rumsfeld v. Forum for Academic & Institutional Rights, Inc., 547 U.S. 47 (2006).

Rust v. Sullivan, 500 U.S. 173 (1991). Brief for the Respondent at 13 (Nos. 89–1391, 89–1392).

Scheidler v. National Organization for Women, Inc., 547 U.S. 9 (2006).

Shaw v. Hunt, 517 U.S 899 (1996).

Sheridan v. E.I. DuPont de Nemours, 100 F. 3d 1061 (3d Cir. 1996).

Stenberg v. Carhart, 530 U.S. 914 (2000).

Tennessee v. Lane, 541 U.S. 509 (2004).

Tinker v. Des Moines Independent Community School District, 303 U.S. 503 (1969).

United States v. Lopez, 514 U.S. 549 (1995).

United States v. Morrison, 529 U.S. 598 (2000).

Washington v. Recuenco, 200 U.S. 212 (2006).

Winkelman v. Parma City School District, 127 S. Ct. 1994 (2007).

Ex-Prisoners' Re-Entry: An Emerging Frontier and a Social Work Challenge

Ram A. Cnaan
Jeffrey Draine
Beverly Frazier
Jill W. Sinha

BACKGROUND

The statistics regarding incarceration in America during the past 20 years indicate soaring numbers of people in prisons and jails. At year's end 2004, state prisons housed 1,244,311 individuals and federal prisons housed 170,535, more than 1.4 million people in total. In addition, at mid-year 2004, 713,990 inmates were held in the nation's local jails. Overall, 2,135,901 different individuals were held as prisoners in federal or state prisons or in local jails in 2004. Between 1995 and 2004, the incarcerated population grew by an average of 3.4 percent annually (U.S. Department of Justice, Bureau of Justice Statistics, 2006). From 1995 to 2004, the number of jail inmates per 100,000 U.S. residents rose from 193 to 243. These numbers combined suggest a very bleak picture: by 2004 nearly 7 million people (3.2 % of U.S. adult residents), or 1 in every 31 adults, were on probation, in jail or prison, or on parole. Put differently, when one sits in a bus or train car, there is a strong likelihood that at least one passenger was previously incarcerated. In any drive to work one is likely to observe or drive next to an ex-prisoner who is still unadjusted to life in the community.

As a society we have moved toward a vindictive and more harshly punitive approach in dealing with lawbreakers (Austin, Bruce, Carroll, McCall, & Richards., 2001; Beckett, 2001; Garland, 2001; King & Mauer, 2002; Mauer, 2000; Tonry, 1999). In the past three decades, politicians, following or at times leading the sentiments of voters, took away the sentencing discretion of judges by legislating mandatory sentences. Terms such as "truth in sentencing" and "three strikes and you are out" captured and dominated public discourse, which led to new sentencing policies (Ditton & Wilson, 1999). For example, in 1988, George H. W. Bush used the case of Willie Horton to demolish the Michael Dukakis campaign and win the election. When Willie Horton was paroled in Massachusetts, his release papers carried the signature of the Commonwealth's Governor, Michael Dukakis. Soon after his release, he was arrested and convicted for another case of rape and murder. George W. H. Bush's message was "keep them longer in prison and we will be safer" (Vidich, 1990). Voters are assumed to agree overwhelmingly that criminals should be locked up thus setting the tone for stricter sentencing and even stricter parole possibilities (Roberts, 1992). Similarly, television programs and movies portrayed the judicial system as weak and overly sympathetic to criminals at the expense of innocent citizens. Maybe the iconic symbol of this era was the *Dirty Harry* series portraying Clint Eastwood as a police detective going after ruthless, if not psychotic, criminals that the criminal justice system let free.

The changes in sentencing resulting in longer prison terms and increased numbers of prisoners led to the need for more and larger correctional facilities. Some states turned to the private sector for assistance; today, several decades later, the "prison industry" continues to boom (Hooks, Mosher, Rotolo & Lobao, 2004; Riveland, 1999; Schlosser, 1998). Communities that lost their manufacturing base are reviving their economies through prison reconstruction and maintenance, leading to prisons in less populated or less desirable parts of the country. One of the consequences of this is that anyone sentenced to state or federal prisons stands a good chance of being transferred to a prison hours away from his or her original community which, in turn, breaks ties with relatives and friends.

There is an imbalance between the expenses of long-term punishment and the cost of rehabilitation (Davey, 1995). For example, the cost of holding one felon in prison is estimated at $22,300 a year (State of Maryland: Governor's Interagency Council on Homelessness, 2005). This cost outweighs many available community alternatives (Garland, 2001). However, the American politic until now, has appeared willing to pay a lot to get harsh punishments and keep felons tucked in prisons.

The cost of imprisonment has ballooned: according to Austin and colleagues (2001), in 1998, the annual amount of public money spent on prisons alone was $35 billion dollars; by 2001, the figure reached $44 billion dollars (up from $9 billion in 1982). Overall, the number of criminal justice system employees grew 86 percent between 1982 and 2003. The total per capita expenditure for each justice function increased between 1982 and 2003, with corrections having the largest per capita increase—423 percent (Hughes, 2006). Meanwhile, data from 1996 show that of the $22 billion spent that year on state prisons for adults, only 6 percent was used to prepare prisoners for life outside prison. These programs include vocational training, life-skills training, educational programs, social activities, psychological treatments, and recreation. Many programs under these names are atrophied shells of their past potential for effectiveness and often serve to control prisons. As a result, even for many prisoners the term "rehabilitation" has fallen into disrepute (LIFERS, 2004).

In addition, the stiff sentences of the past several decades have sent and kept many members of our society in prison for longer periods and have not prepared the 97 percent who will eventually return to the community

(Massachusetts Public Health Association, 2003; Travis, 2001). The country now faces growing numbers of ex-prisoners returning to the community each year after significant time behind bars. Many ex-prisoners learned to survive in prison by "toughening up" and adopting a worldview that helps them cope, but this same worldview is inadequate and unproductive for community reintegration.

Our popular public view of prisoners is that they enjoy life in prison and have too much leisure; we want them to suffer and be miserable (Jacobs, 2004; Whitman, 2003). Contrary to the "country club" myth that suggests prisoners spend their time watching television and using fitness centers, life in prison is difficult and dangerous. Most people leave prison hoping never to return, determined to stay out of trouble and be model citizens. Some dream of restored lives as spouses or parents, or with their significant others (Visher & Travis, 2003).

Daily, about 1,600 prisoners are released from prison. Estimates indicate that this number represents an increase of nearly six times the number of prisoners released in 1980 (Harrison & Karberg, 2003). Each one needs help adjusting to life in the community. Rates of reincarceration suggest that successful re-entry is difficult at best. Preventing reincarceration will become one of American society's greatest challenges for the twenty-first century.

In the next section, we try to provide a broad picture our nation's prisoners. This is followed by a section regarding the impact of prison life on individuals. We also chronicle the hardships of re-entry and its impact on the community. We conclude with a section on how to facilitate re-entry and the role that social work can play in this important frontier.

WHO IS IMPRISONED IN THE U.S.?

Most prisoners are young people (median age 34) with an estimated 57 percent of inmates under the age of 35 in 2001 (U.S. Department of Justice, Bureau of Justice Statistics, 2006). Sixty-eight percent of state prison inmates do not have a high school diploma and have few vocational skills (Harlow, 2003). Many prisoners were unemployed or only partially employed prior to their arrest or held positions earning less than $1,000 a month.

Another cause for concern is not only the sheer number of incarcerations, but the proportion of minorities who are incarcerated. The chances of black and Latino persons being incarcerated are dramatically higher than those of white persons (Blumstein & Beck, 1999; Marbley & Ferguson, 2005). Ethnic minorities, notably black and Latino, comprise 64 percent of the state prison population and 59 percent of the federal prison population, but comprise only about 20 percent of the total U.S. population. Incarceration rates indicate that more than one-quarter of black men (28.5%) will spend time in prison at some point in their lives compared to a lifetime risk of 4.4 percent for white males (Bonzcar & Beck, 2003). In addition to minorities, poor people are arrested and convicted more often than people with greater resources. Thus, the combination of race and class can be a strong predictor of who is found in our prisons and jails, and this reality affects the re-entry process.

In our nation's jails, women make up an increasing proportion of inmates, 12.7 percent of the population in 2005 (up from 10.2 percent in 1995). However in state and federal prisons women accounted for 7 percent of all prisoners, up from 6.1 percent at year's end 1995 (U.S. Department of Justice, Bureau of Justice Statistics, 2006). Most women prisoners are also minority women. Although the involvement of women in crime is on the rise, men are still the overwhelming majority of prisoners.

Ditton (1999) reported that 16.2 percent of state prison inmates and 7.2 percent of federal prison inmates are estimated to have psychiatric treatment histories. Among those in local jails or probation, estimates indicate that 16 percent have psychiatric treatment histories. With the deinstitutionalization of mental health hospitals and the trend of harsh and determinate sentences, the proportion of violent prisoners decreased (Caplow & Simon, 1999). Lamb and Weinberger (1998) suggested that "it appears that a greater proportion of mentally ill persons are arrested compared with the general population" (p. 483). Draine, Salzer, Culhane, & Hadley (2002) suggested that the core problem is poverty. They found that

> the impact of mental illness on crime, unemployment, and homelessness appears to be much smaller than that implied by much of the psychiatric services literature. Poverty moderates the relationship between serious mental illness and social problems. Factors related to poverty include lack of education, problems with employment, substance abuse, and a low likelihood of prosocial attachments. (p. 565) .

The proportion of people who test positive for substance abuse when arrested has also increased. Once incarcerated, estimates of all prisoners who are using alcohol or drugs are as high as two-thirds to three-quarters (Primm, Osher, & Gomez, 2005). In most prisons, drugs are easily accessible and most attempts to eradicate drug use in prisons have failed. Thus, one of the consistent factors affecting both prison life and re-entry is the reality of substance abuse. Rates of relapse of drug use for ex-prisoners upon release are very high. Often, drugs are readily available to the ex-incarcerated while treatment options are limited (Mumola, 1999).

Due to harsher sentences, recent cohorts of ex-prisoners have a higher proportion who have served five or more years. Thus, in the larger picture of re-entry, current and near-future cohorts of newly released ex-prisoners are larger, include more people with histories of violence and/or drug abuse, and have served longer sentences. Such individuals are likely to face greater challenges to re-entry and to require appropriate reintegration services.

The emerging picture is that most people exiting prison have fewer resources in human and social capital as well as financial capital than most citizens have (Draine,Wolff, Jacoby, Hartwell & DuClor, 2005; Wolff & Draine, 2004). Over time, the number of people incarcerated has grown, especially among minorities and poor people. The time spent in prison has also increased and prison life has become harsher. As such, prison has a lasting impact on the ex-prisoners.

LIFE IN PRISON AND ITS IMPACT ON PRISONERS

Once arrested, the individual is taken to a local jail until sentencing occurs. After sentencing, depending on the verdict, some are released, whereas others who serve a short time remain in a local jail. Local jails are usually within the same city where the crime occurred. In this case, relatives are able to visit and maintain contact. Visits, however, are limited and closely supervised. Convicts who receive sentences of two or more years are incarcerated in state or federal prisons. In these cases, prisoners may be transferred first to a processing prison and later to a permanent prison. In most cases, state and federal prisons are located hundreds of miles away, often in areas that are sparsely populated and do not have public transportation. Some states build large prison facilities to house "out of state" prisoners, known as "interstate transfer" (Lawrence & Travis, 2004). Thus, many prisoners are transferred away from their home communities and their natural social networks. There-fore, visitation is time-consuming, difficult, and costly for relatives and friends (Christian, 2005). Because the majority of prisoners come from poor families, the farther away the prison from the family residence, the lower the chances are for frequency of visitation.

Being imprisoned far from one's home makes telephone calls a natural means of communication. Almost all prisons provide telephone opportunities for prisoners to call home or elsewhere according to a certain schedule. However, the cost of calls to and from prisons can be exorbitant. Many poor families may lack access to telephones and those with phones may not be able to afford the cost of collect calls from prisons. As a result, many families reluctantly or willingly block collect calls and thus further estrange prisoners (Hairston, 2001).

The U. S. Department of Justice (2000) reported that more than half of prisoners (54 percent for females and 57 percent for males) have not been visited by their children since entering prison. Bates, Archibald, and Wills (2001) provided a comprehensive review of the obstacles to prison visitation and communication between prisoners and their families of origin. Although 15 percent of couples stay together during the prison term, only 3–5 percent are still together one year after the spouse's release. In other words, the spouse's absence due to incarceration endangers marriage, but readjustment after release also takes its toll on the marriage.

Life inside prison forces people to develop emotional survival tactics. Within prison, there is a complex social hierarchy to be navigated. Unlike life in the community, life in prison is highly regimented and the individual has little control over daily choices. Waking up, eating, recreation, and showering are ordered by the prison's administration with little flexibility for personal preferences (Haney, 2001). Thus, emotions must be carefully guarded and even more carefully expressed. Men and women become de-individuated, knowing their place in the system by their address, such as "D Ward," or intake number. This culture is replicated and reinforced by jail and prison management policies to the point that even the act of being identified as having significant health issues, such as mental illness, can have multifaceted implications for power and control within the correctional setting. This significantly complicates the quality of diagnosis, treatment, and rehabilitation of behavioral health disorders in jails and prisons.

In response, the prison culture calls for inmates to be tough, showing only a restricted set of emotions. Inmates are expected to be strong, impenetrable, and capable of protecting themselves from abuse by other prisoners and prison authorities. Quickly enough, the new prisoner learns that life in the outside world has little relevance for survival and functioning inside prison. Violence is virtually necessary to cope in an environment in which survival is often dependent on demonstrating to others who would rob, assault, or rape you that you are more dangerous than they are (Gilligan & Lee, 2004). One fear that most inmates face is aggressive sexual assault by other prisoners (Bosworth & Carrabine, 2003; Wooden & Parker, 1982). Consequently, most prisoners develop an emotional coping mechanism of apathy.

Unlike European countries where prisoners are allowed conjugal visits and home vacations, American prisoners are deprived of such opportunities for relaxation or intimacy. This may be related to the high rates of sexual assault within prisons. Beck and Hughes (2005) estimated that over the past 20 years, the total number of inmates who have been sexually assaulted likely exceeds one million. In 2003, President George W. Bush signed into law the Prison Rape Elimination Act (PREA), which requires correctional institutions to provide data on sexual assaults within their respective facilities, yet most victims prefer to conceal their victimization for fear of retaliation and further abuse.

In addition to emotional health, the physical health of many people in prison is also problematic when compared with the general population. Incarcerated populations are disproportionately affected by diseases such as tuberculosis (TB), hepatitis B and C, and HIV, which are commonly spread through sexual contact with other individuals, sharing needles, and eating with the same utensils (Hammett, Harmon, & Rhodes, 2002). According to the World Health Organization (2006), the rate of TB in incarcerated populations is reportedly up to 100 times greater than that of the general population. Salive, Vlahov, and Brewer (2003) found positive associations between HIV and TB in their sample of 698 male inmates in a Maryland correctional institution because TB spreads more rapidly to HIV-positive inmates. Not surprisingly, the prevalence of AIDS infection is approximately five times higher in state and federal prisons than among the general U.S. population (Dean, Lansky, & Fleming, 2002; Krebs & Simmons, 2002).

Life in American prisons debilitates and dehumanizes inmates (Bonta & Gendreau, 1990; Haney, 2001; Huey & Mcnulty, 2005). Rehabilitation efforts are limited and tough and aggressive stances toward inmates are seen as desirable (Cullen, Fisher, & Applegate, 2000). The general emerging picture indicates that the thousands of people who are released from prison daily in the United States are faced with the challenges of re-entry such as re-establishing contact and relationship with family, friends, and employers, finding stable housing, income, and possibly fighting addictions or major health concerns. Given their stay in prison and any trauma that they experienced, and given the circumstances that preceded their incarceration, which most likely included being a racial minority, and having less education and fewer financial resources, their odds of successful reintegration into the community are daunting. Contact with relatives and friends may be tenuous, and many are sick, poor, and possibly drug dependent, not to mention the emotional scars they may be carrying with them.

THE HARDSHIP OF RE-ENTRY AND ITS IMPACT ON COMMUNITY

The massive burden of imprisonment and re-entry over the past two decades has significantly weakened the capacity of many communities, especially some of the most vulnerable, to carry out successful civic life. The key tasks of communities, such as providing a sense of security and pride, a healthy environment for families, jobs, and open exchanges and support, are hampered when large numbers of the population are recycling in and out of correctional facilities and carrying with them the lasting consequences of incarceration.

Given the expense of running prisons, as well as the high cost to human dignity and capability, it is in our national interest that ex-prisoners successfully reintegrate into the community and avoid recidivism. The transition from prison to the community can be tough and frustrating. One needs to unlearn the survival skills learned in prison, take responsibility for his or her criminal past, which often includes substance abuse, and make amends with close relatives who are hurt and distrustful. Comforts or escapes, through sex, alcohol, or drugs are available and tempting. Thus, the community offers disincentives for successful re-entry. Not surprisingly, about a third of incoming prisoners did nothing more than fail their parole conditions, given that half of all parolees fail to meet these conditions (Petersilia, 1999).

Nearly two-thirds (63%) of those released from state and federal prisons may be expected to be rearrested for a felony, a serious misdemeanor, or a technical parole violation within three years of their release. About half (47%) are reconvicted and about two-fifths (41%) return to prison. Unpacking these statistics shows that younger ex-prisoners with more extensive criminal careers are more likely to become recidivists (Travis & Visher, 2005). Consequently, unsuccessful re-entry must be viewed not only as an issue for law enforcement—when the individual becomes involved in new criminal activity, new victimization, or missed parole visits—but unsuccessful re-entry should also be viewed as a major social and communal burden that requires the professional attention and skills of the social work profession. This is especially important given the geographic concentration of arrests and re-entries in a few city neighborhoods, which creates neighborhood-level effects for the extent of incarceration and has implications for re-entry (Clear, Rose, & Ryder, 2001).

Typical prisoners leave prison with less than $100, the clothes in which they were arrested, a small package of personal belongings, and a bus ticket to the original place of arrest. When they reach their destination, many must report to a parole officer, register with the sheriff, report to welfare agencies, register for work, and meet other similar requirements. Most have lost their social security cards and their driver's licenses are no longer valid. Replacing documents and establishing residences involves bureaucratic red tape as well as payments and transportation that are often beyond the means of the ex-prisoners. Ex-prisoners are often unskilled in asking for help in public offices, and they are often denied assistance even when entitled to it.

When searching for housing and jobs, ex-prisoners are rarely welcomed (Pager, 2003). The stigma they carry is permanent and must be made public on applications. Many people and organizations shy away from individuals with a criminal history because it suggests that the person is untrustworthy or unreliable (Ramon & Travis, 2004; Solomon, Johnson, Travis, & McBride, 2004). A common viewpoint is that ex-prisoners cannot change and will revert to a life of crime, and for the individual ex-prisoner, these attitudes spell double jeopardy. Consequently, few community programs, employers, or landlords will assist them. In response, ex-prisoners may resort to the skills they developed in conning those around them to survive.

For a large percentage of prisoners, life before imprisonment involved drug use and a lifestyle of instant gratification: Approximately six out of ten prisoners report using drugs at least once in the month prior to arrest (Ditton, 1999). Upon release, drugs are easily accessible while detox and rehabilitation programs are not (Petersilia, 2003). Most ex-prisoners are ineligible for substance abuse programs. The people with whom the ex-prisoner uses drugs often support crime as a way of life because crime is often the quickest route to cash. Finding a social support system that is crime-resistant and enabling is a major challenge for most ex-prisoners.

Some ex-prisoners wish to enter drug-treatment programs but they must obtain Medicaid to be eligible, which means completing the application process and waiting for approval. Others leave prison with health problems and find that once released they are ineligible for health care or must wait a long time to be approved for Medicaid (Morrissey et al., 2006). Furthermore, even if Medicaid is approved, myriad cultural and organizational disconnects between correctional, behavioral health, and social service systems may serve to further isolate ex-prisoners with multiple problems (Wilson & Draine, 2006).

Prison provided an environment with a bed and food—necessities that ex-prisoners are very suddenly without. Many states bar ex-prisoners from applying for housing assistance, or impose several years' waiting time before being eligible to apply. In many cases the alternative is life on the street or in a shelter, especially in cities where the housing market is tight and the cost of housing is high (Petersilia, 2003). Data from Los Angeles and San Francisco suggest that daily, 30 to 50 percent of all people under parole supervision are homeless (Travis, Solomon, & Waul, 2001). Metraux and Culhane (2004) found that at least 11 percent of people released from New York State prisons to New York City from 1995 to 1998 entered a homeless shelter within two years—more than half of these in the first month after release. Most landlords are prohibited from renting to ex-prisoners who were convicted on drug or violent charges. Many more employers and landlords personally elect not to deal with this population and reject ex-prisoners' applications upon discovering a criminal history (Bushway, 2000).

Twelve states have implemented legal barriers to full citizenship for ex-prisoners. In Florida, Kentucky, and Virginia, ex-felons permanently lose their right to vote. Nine other states have such restrictions in place for two or more years. Most states temporarily prohibit prisoners and parolees from voting (Uggen, Manza, & Thompson, 2006). These prohibitions infringe on ex-prisoners' civil rights and send the message that they are outside the realm of citizenry. Many states permanently prohibit ex-offenders from election to any public office.

Even more punitive, most states impose restrictions and prohibit the hiring of ex-prisoners in fields such as law, education, real estate, nursing, and medicine. Six states permanently bar ex-prisoners from holding any public employment. Studies show that time spent in prison lowers the individual's earning capacity (Kling, 1999). Jobs that prisoners fulfilled during incarceration are mostly unsuitable for the market demand. Prisoners can only find low-paid, unskilled jobs if they can find any job at all.

As such, the chances of an ex-prisoner obtaining a job that will enable him or her to live with dignity are quite slim. These conditions tend to isolate ex-prisoners from vocation-based earnings and support the temptation for illegal cash-earning activities.

As suggested earlier, the level of separation from family and friends during incarceration poses a major barrier to ex-prisoners as they go back to the community. Often, by the time prisoners near release, they have become strangers in their own neighborhood. Indeed, many find they have been replaced by newer boyfriends or girlfriends. In many cases, families and children have formed strong relationships to new individuals who may function as de facto parents (Beatty, 1997). Children may be quite attached to the de facto parent and consider him or her to be their "real parent." Those who wish to restore family ties find it disappointing that their children have grown and many decisions were made without their parental involvement.

Female prisoners are of special concern because 65 percent have a child under age 18. More than 1.3 million children in the United States have a mother who is incarcerated or under parole supervision. Men in prison and prior to incarceration often do not have close contact with their children; women generally keep in touch and desire to be a regular part of their children's lives (Greenfield & Snell, 1999). In addition to the challenge of staying connected with children during imprisonment and reconnecting with them after prison, a huge difficulty is the care of children who do not have other caretakers when a mother is sentenced. Often children are declared eligible for adoption when a mother is sentenced, especially if the child is young, and no father or grandparent steps in to claim guardianship. Given the growing rate of incarceration for females with dependent children, this is a grave issue for the social work profession and society.

Ex-prisoners are not the only victims of unsuccessful re-entry: children suffer when their released parent cannot reintegrate into the family and community. From the perspective of a child, this adult has routinely broken laws and disappeared from his or her life (Gabel, 1992). Nearly one and a half million children under the age of 18 have a parent incarcerated in a state or federal prison (Gabel & Johnston, 1995). Many children experience a parent's incarceration in a local jail for a short time. Children's psychological well-being is jeopardized both when a parent is incarcerated and when the parent returns.

Young men of minority ethnic groups go in and out of prisons disproportionately. Their communities suffer as well. The communities in which these young men and women live lose an important segment of their members to jail and prison (Mauer & Chesney-Lind, 2002). Consequently, marital and family lives are significantly interrupted. Young women may choose not to marry someone who is unlikely to be around or who cannot provide a living wage to the family. The safety that was supposed to be gained by sending active and potential criminals to prison is compromised in neighborhoods where disproportionate numbers of friends, relatives, husbands, brothers, and fathers are incarcerated or are ex-prisoners. Despite the known social and financial benefits of traditional marriage for children and spouses, the punitive effects of long sentences and incarceration make long-term consensual, legal, and binding relationships unattractive to potential female spouses. In contrast, being a single working parent and/or using subsidized care and benefits for children are financially more rewarding.

As noted, incarcerations and re-entry are not evenly distributed among communities. Certain states, such as California and Texas, absorb a high proportion of people exiting prison. Similarly, in cities, certain neighborhoods experience a far greater proportion of people who are arrested, imprisoned, and return. Often, such neighborhoods have similar compositions of ethnic minorities, who earn low incomes and lack political clout. Compounding the problem, these neighborhoods often lack the formal and economic infrastructure, employment opportunities, and political organization to facilitate services needed if returning ex-prisoners are to successfully reintegrate (Clear, Rose, & Ryder, 2001).

On the positive side, many individuals who are released under parole have help in their transition from prison to community under a designated parole officer. However, as the number of people released from prison increases, the budget for probation and parole officers has decreased. The ratio of parolees to parole officers has therefore increased dramatically. Today, parole officers carry high caseloads, diminishing their ability to attend to the needs of these individuals (Massachusetts Public Health Association, 2003).

People who complete their full sentence and are not paroled are released without any formal supervision. More than half of those released from maximum and medium security prisons are released directly to the community without any contact or supervision (Pihel, 2002). Without formal supervision, these individuals may seem to be "free" and unbounded, but are often ill-prepared to live in the community and are unaware of their eligibility for a variety of services.

HOW TO HELP IN RE-ENTRY:
THE CHALLENGES AHEAD

Dealing with ex-prisoners and making the process of re-entry more successful is one of American society's greatest challenges for the twenty-first century. It is in the best interest of our society to reduce crime in the community and to lower the rates of incarceration. However, how to achieve these goals is complex and costly. In this section, we limit the discussion to what social work can do to make this issue a national priority and what it can do to assist.

In the 1970s, at the leading edge of the current incarceration binge, the profession of social work abdicated its historical role as an agent for rehabilitation and reintegration of people leaving jails and prisons. Social workers have since allowed professional criminal justice workers to capture this role, and to refocus this work toward the safety and security of society and away from the traditional values of the social work profession in empowering individuals and building community capacity (Gumz, 2004). The first task is to reclaim work with prisoners—not just those re-entering the community, but all prisoners—as a focus of social work practice. If social work focuses on ex-prisoners and re-entry, social workers should ensure that they do not also normalize "re-entry" as a service model decontexualized from the policy issue of removal and mass incarceration (Clear, Rose & Ryder, 2001).

Ex-prisoners are most likely to have adjustment problems and commit new offenses in the first six months after release (Nelson, Deess, & Allen, 1999). New crimes committed by ex-prisoners place greater burdens on parole and police officers and can be devastating to family members and individuals in the community. In addition, the continued cost of housing new and returning prisoners is high and rising. Compared to these costs, the effort put into preventing recidivism, particularly during the critical first six months, is worthwhile for ethical and financial reasons. The new social frontier of reintegration will challenge American society to constrain public and private funds to deal with this epidemic (Petersilia, 2001). Social work needs to be ready with trained professionals and intervention programs to serve the ex-prisoners and the communities to which they return (Petersilia, 1999).

Although public sentiment indicates that prisons should focus on punishing rather than educating, treating, rehabilitating or transforming the people we call criminals, it will benefit society if prisoners are prepared for making the transition to the community. Reintegrating requires a psychological shift as well as the acquisition of new skills. Most prisons offer few rehabilitation programs and the available programs are ineffective, oversubscribed and are not integrated with the outside world. However, pre-release interventions may facilitate more successful reintegration. A few studies have indicated a positive prognosis for ex-prisoners when they participated in pre-release programs. Wexler, DeLeon, Thomas, Kressel, & Peters (1999) highlighted the improved chances of remaining drug free with ex-prisoners who completed both in-prison and post-prison drug-rehabilitation programs.

Here we focus on two prevalent issues that ex-prisoners face in reintegration, namely, housing and adjustment. Not all types of housing are appropriate for all ex-prisoners in the stage immediately after release. The switch from a fully structured and drug-limited prison environment, to one with little or no structure, combined with the availability of drugs, and the stresses of becoming self-sufficient and getting reacquainted with family and friends is often too difficult for ex-prisoners to successfully navigate.

A living environment that promotes support in relationships, finding employment, and managing finances, along with gradual independence, helps a great many ex-prisoners adjust to society (Taxman, 2005). Many ex-prisoners have routinely experienced hurt, betrayal, and loss in their past. Until deep-seated emotions of betrayal and anger are addressed, many ex-prisoners cannot sustain healthy relationships with loved ones (Travis, Solomon, & Waul, 2001). No matter how toughened ex-prisoners are, in their most intimate self, they each need love, appreciation, and healthy companionship to heal the pain or betrayal that they have experienced.

These two examples suggest how, along with an appropriate counseling and drug-free environment, case management that is tailored to meet the needs of ex-prisoners can promote successful reintegration and self-sufficiency. Every ex-prisoner demands many hours of care and presents unique problems possibly including housing, drug rehabilitation, employment, reconnecting with children, parents and/or spouse, help in acquiring documents, on-going legal obligations, transportation, and medical services. Such intensive care is possible only when a caseworker deals with a small number of ex-prisoners.

As evidenced in drug rehabilitation, successful programs for female ex-prisoners look different from successful programs for male ex-prisoners (Hser, Huang, & Teruya, 2004). In interviews with re-entry providers who served males, they distrusted men who were released from prison to act appropriately around women and often banned contact with women in the early stages of release and reintegration (Cnaan & Sinha, 2003). In some cases, even spouses and fiancées were included in this restriction until the men could demonstrate healthy emotional choices. Even programs that allowed contact between male ex-prisoners and women did not allow co-ed programs and viewed co-ed contact as a potential recipe for failure to successful reintegration. For women ex-prisoners, the ability to have contact or cohabitation with dependent children is a significant and immediate concern.

Another obstacle for successful re-entry is the lack of coordination regarding services for ex-prisoners. Despite the variety and availability of services, including drug rehabilitation, shelter, GED training, computer skills, and vocational skills programs, connecting with these services, or having them ill suited for the ex-prison population is problematic. Without well-advertised and relevant services, programs were either forced to provide their own services, spend a lot of time finding relevant services, or risk losing ex-prisoners to other lifestyles because they could not get the necessary supportive services. Social work professionals have a vast experience and expertise that can be harnessed to assist ex-prisoners, their families and their communities, to better coordinate the network of available services as well as assess any needed services to be developed.

CONCLUSION

As we have presented, ex-prisoners today have been incarcerated for longer periods, possess less education and fewer job skills, and are often plagued by physical and mental health problems, and/or drug addiction. They are often members of ethnic minorities and come from poor families that find it hard to support them or keep in touch with them. Longer prison terms also imply living under psychological duress and having to develop emotional coping mechanisms that affect their ability to sustain healthy relationships or employment when they are released.

Despite the clear long-term benefits of supporting reintegration, the public system that is expected to help ex-prisoners is overburdened, and society at large is suspicious of them and makes it known they are not welcome in jobs and communities. As in the past, the social work profession should defend, support, and facilitate the fuller participation of the most marginalized populations in society. In this era, the social work profession must embrace the growing population of ex-prisoners by advocating on their behalf, educating society of their unique needs and challenges, and developing appropriately coordinated, relevant, and accessible programs to assist their successful reintegration into families, communities, sustainable living-wage employment, and civic duties.

REFERENCES

Austin, J., Bruce, M. A., Carroll, L., McCall, P. L., & Richards, S. C. (2001). The use of incarceration in the United States. *Critical Criminology, 10*, 17–41.

Bates, R., Archibald, J., & Wills, S. (2001). *Improving outcomes for children and families of incarcerated parents*. Chicago: University of Illinois at Chicago, Jane Addams School of Social Work, Center for Social Policy and Research and Chicago Legal Aid to Incarcerated Mothers.

Beatty, C. (1997). *Parents in prison: Children in crisis*. Washington, DC: Child Welfare League of America.

Beck, A. J., & Hughes, T. A. (2005). *Sexual violence reported by correctional authorities, 2004*. Washington, DC: U.S. Department of Justice.

Beckett, K. (2001). Governing social marginality: Welfare, incarceration, and the transformation of state policy. *Punishment & Society, 3*, 43–59.

Blumstein, A., & Beck, A. J. (1999). Population growth in U.S. prisons, 1980–1996. In M. Tonry & J. Petersilia (Eds.), *Prisons* (pp. 17–61). Chicago: University of Chicago Press.

Bonta, J., & Gendreau, P. (1990). Reexamining the cruel and unusual punishment of prison life. *Law and Human Behavior, 14*, 347–372.

Bonzcar, T., & Beck, A. (2003). *Lifetime likelihood of going to state or federal prison*. Washington, DC: U.S. Department of Justice. Bureau of Justice Statistics Special Report, (NCJ-160092).

Bosworth, M., & Carrabine, E. (2003). Reassessing resistance: Race, gender and sexuality in prison. *Punishment & Society, 3*, 501–515.

Bushway, S. (2000). The stigma of criminal history record in the labor market. In J. P. May (Ed.), *Building violence: How America's rush to incarcerate creates more violence* (pp. 142–148). Thousand Oaks, CA: Sage.

Caplow, T., & Simon, J. (1999). Understanding prison policy and population trends. *Crime and Justice, 26*, 63–120.

Christian, J. (2005). Riding the bus: Barriers to prison visitation and family management strategies. *Journal of Contemporary Criminal Justice, 21*, 31–48.

Clear, T. R., Rose, D. R., & Ryder, J. A. (2001). Incarceration and the community: The problem of removing and returning offenders. *Crime and Delinquency, 47*, 335–351.

Cnaan, R. A., & Sinha, J. W. (2003). *Back into the fold: Helping prisoners reconnect through faith*. Baltimore: Annie E. Casey Foundation.

Cullen, F. T., Fisher, B. S., & Applegate, B. K. (2000). Public opinion about punishment and corrections. *Crime and Justice: A Review of Research, 27*, 1–79.

Davey, J. D. (1995). *The new social contract: America's journey from welfare state to police state*. New York: Greenwood.

Dean, H. D., Lansky, A., & Fleming, P. L. (2002). HIV surveillance methods for the incarcerated population. *AIDS Education and Prevention, 14*, 65–74.

Ditton, P. M. (1999). *Mental health and treatment of inmates and probationers.* Washington, DC: U.S. Department of Justice, Bureau of Justice Statistics (NCJ174463).

Ditton, P. M., & Wilson, D. J. (1999). *Truth in sentencing in state prisons.* Washington, DC: U.S. Department of Justice, Bureau of Justice Statistics (NCJ 170032).

Draine, J., Salzer, M. S., Culhane, D. P., & Hadley, T. R. (2002). Role of social disadvantage in crime, joblessness, and homelessness among persons with serious mental illness. *Psychiatric Services, 53*, 565–573.

Draine, J., Wolff, N., Jacoby, J. E., Hartwell, S., & DuClos, C. (2005). Understanding community re-entry of former prisoners with mental illness: A conceptual guide to guide new research. *Behavioral Health Sciences and the Law, 23*, 689–707.

Gabel, K. (1992). Behavioral problems in sons of incarcerated or otherwise absent fathers: The issue of separation. *Family Process, 31*, 303–314.

Gabel, K., & Johnston, D. (1995). *Children of incarcerated parents.* New York: Lexington Books.

Garland, D. (2001). *The culture of control: Crime and social order in contemporary society.* Chicago: University of Chicago Press.

Gilligan, J., & Lee, B. (2004). Beyond the prison paradigm: From provoking violence to preventing it by creating "anti-prisons" (residential colleges and therapeutic communities). *Annals of the New York Academy of Sciences, 1036*, 300–324.

Greenfield, L. A., & Snell, T. L. (1999). *Women offenders.* Washington, DC: U.S. Department of Justice, Bureau of Justice Statistics (NCJ 175688).

Gumz, E. J. (2004). American social work, corrections and restorative justice: An appraisal. *International Journal of Offender Therapy and Comparative Criminology, 48*, 449–460.

Hairston, C. F. (2001). Fathers in prison: Responsible fatherhood and responsible public policies. *Marriage & Family Review, 32*, 111–135.

Hammett, T. H., Harmon, P., & Rhodes, W. (2002). The burden of infectious diseases among inmates of and releasees from U.S. correctional facilities, 1997. *American Journal of Public Health, 92*, 1789–1794.

Haney, C. (2001). The psychological impact of incarceration: Implications for post-prison adjustment. In *From prison to home: The effect of incarceration and re-entry on children, families and communities.* Washington, DC: Working papers, the Urban Institute. Retrieved October 20, 2006, from: http://aspe.hhs.gov/hsp/prison2home02/haney.pdf.

Harlow, C. W. (2003). *Education and correctional populations.* Washington, DC: U.S. Department of Justice, Bureau of Justice Statistics (NCJ195670).

Harrison, P. M., & Karberg, J. C. (2003). *Prison and jail prisoners at midyear 2002.* Washington, DC: Bureau of Justice Statistics, U.S. Department of Justice.

Hooks, G., Mosher, C., Rotolo, T., & Lobao, L. (2004). The prison industry: Carceral expansion and employment in U.S. Counties, 1969–1994. *Social Science Quarterly, 85*, 37–57.

Hser, Y., Huang, Y., & Teruya, C. (2004). Gender differences in treatment outcomes over a three-year period: A path model analysis. *Journal of Drug Issues, 34*, 419–439.

Huey, M. P., & Mcnulty, T. L. (2005). Institutional conditions and prison suicide: Conditional effects of deprivation and overcrowding. *The Prison Journal, 85,* 490–514.

Hughes, K. A. (2006). *Justice expenditure and employment in the United States, 2003.* Washington, DC: U.S. Department of Justice, Office of Justice Program. Retrieved July 2nd, 2006 from: http://www.ojp.usdoj.gov/bjs/pub/pdf/jeeus03.pdf

Jacobs, J. B. (2004). Prison reform amid the ruins of prisoners' rights. In M. Tonry (Ed.). *Future of imprisonment: Essays in honor of Norval Morris* (pp. 179–198). New York: Oxford University Press.

King, R. S., & Mauer, M. (2002). *State sentencing and corrections policy in an era of fiscal retrenchment.* Washington, DC: The Sentencing Project.

Kling, J. (1999). *The effect of prison sentence length on the subsequent employment and earnings of a criminal defendant.* Princeton, NJ: Princeton University, Woodrow Wilson School Economics Discussion Paper.

Krebs, C., & Simmons, M. (2002). Intraprison HIV transmission: An assessment of whether it occurs, how it occurs, and who is at risk. *AIDS Education and Prevention, 14*(Suppl. B), 53–64.

Lamb, H. R., & Weinberger, L. E. (1998). Persons with severe mental illness in jails and prisons: A review. *Psychiatric Services, 49,* 483–492.

Lawrence, S., & Travis, J. (2004). *The new landscape of imprisonment: Mapping America's prison expansion.* Washington, DC: Urban Institute.

LIFERS Public Safety Steering Committee of the State Correctional Institution at Graterford, Pennsylvania (2004). Ending the culture of street crime. *The Prison Journal, 84,* 48S–68S.

Marbley, A. F., & Ferguson, R. (2005). Responding to prisoner re-entry, recidivism, and incarceration of inmates of color: a call to the communities. *Journal of Black Studies, 35,* 633–649.

Massachusetts Public Health Association (2003). *Correctional health: The missing key to improving the public's health and safety.* Boston: Author. Retrieved May 21, 2006 from: http://www.mphaweb.org/home_correctionalhealth10_03.pdf

Mauer, M. (2000). *The race to incarcerate.* Washington, DC: The Prison Project.

Mauer, M., & Chesney-Lind, M. (2002). *Invisible punishment: The collateral consequences of mass imprisonment.* New York: New Press.

Morrissey, J. P., Steadman, H. J., Dalton, K. M., Cuellar, A. Stiles, P. & Cuddleback, G. S. (2006). Medicaid enrollment and mental health service use following release of jail detainees with severe mental illness. *Psychiatric Services, 57,* 809–815.

Mumola, C. J. (1999). *Substance abuse and treatment: State and federal prisoners, 1997.* Washington, DC: U.S. Department of Justice, Bureau of Justice Statistics (NCJ 172871).

Metraux, S., & Culhane, D. P. (2004). Homeless shelter use and reincarceration following prison release: Assessing the risk. *Criminology & Public Policy, 3,* 139–160.

Nelson, M., Deess, P., & Allen, C. (1999). *The first month out: Post-incarceration experiences in New York City.* New York: Vera Institute of Justice.

Pager, D. (2003). The mark of a criminal record. *American Journal of Sociology, 108,* 937–975.

Petersilia, J. (1999). Parole and prisoner re-entry in the United States. In: M. Tonry & J. Petersilia (Eds.). *Prisons* (pp. 479–529). Chicago: University of Chicago Press.

Petersilia, J. (2001). When prisoners return to the community: Political, economic, and social consequences. *Corrections Management Quarterly, 5*(3), 1–10.

Petersilia, J. (2003). *When prisoners come home: Parole and prisoner re-entry.* New York: Oxford University Press.

Pihel, A. M. (2002). *From cell to street: A plan to supervise inmates after release.* Boston: MassInc (The Massachusetts Institute for a New Commonwealth).

Primm, A. B., Osher, F. C., & Gomez, M. B. (2005). Race and ethnicity, mental health services and cultural competence in the criminal justice system: Are we ready to change? *Community Mental Health Journal, 41*, 557–569.

Ramon, C. G., & Travis, J. (2004). *Taking stock: Housing, homelessness, and prisoner re-entry.* Washington, DC: Urban Institute.

Riveland, C. (1999). Prison management trends, 1975–2005. *Crime and Justice, 26*, 163–203.

Roberts, J. V. (1992). Public opinion, crime, and criminal justice. *Crime and Justice, 16*, 99–180.

Salive, M. E., Vlahov, D., & Brewer, T. F. (1990). Coinfection with tuberculosis and HIV-1 in male prison inmates. *Public Journal Report, 105*, 307–310.

Schlosser, E. (December, 1998). The prison: Industrial complex. *The Atlantic Monthly*, 51–77.

Solomon, A. L., Johnson, K. D., Travis, J., & McBride, E. C. (2004). *From prison to work: The employment dimensions of prisoner re-entry. A report of the Re-entry Roundtable.* Washington, DC: Urban Institute.

State of Maryland: Governor's Interagency Council on Homelessness (2005). *10-years plan to end homelessness.* Baltimore: Author. Retrieved July 2nd, 2006 from: http://www.dhr.state.md.us/transit/pdf/ich-plan.pdf

Taxman, F. S. (2005). Brick walls facing reentering offenders. *International Journal of Comparative and Applied Criminal Justice, 29*, 5–18.

Tonry, M. (1999). Why are U.S. incarceration rates so high? *Crime & Delinquency, 45*, 419–437.

Travis, J. (2001). But they all come back: Rethinking prisoner re-entry. *Corrections Management Quarterly, 5* (3), 23–33.

Travis, J., Solomon, A. L., & Waul, M. (2001). *From prison to home: The dimensions and consequences of prisoner re-entry.* Washington, DC: The Urban institute.

Travis, J., & Visher, C. (2005). *Prisoner re-entry and crime in America.* New York: Cambridge University Press.

Uggen, C., Manza, J., & Thompson, M. (2006). Citizenship, democracy, and the civic reintegration of criminal offenders. *The Annals of the American Academy of Political and Social Science, 605,* 281–310.

U.S. Department of Justice (2000). *Incarcerated parents and their children.* Washington, DC: Author.

U.S. Department of Justice, Bureau of Justice Statistics (2006). *Correction statistics.* Retrieved May 10, 2006 from: http://www.ojp.usdoj.gov/bjs/correct.htm

Vidich, A. J. (1990). American democracy in the late twentieth century: Political rhetorics and mass media. *International Journal of Politics, Culture, and Society, 4*, 5–29.

Visher, C., & Travis, J. (2003). Transitions from prison to community: Understanding individual pathways. *Annual Review of Sociology, 29,* 89–113.

Wexler, H. K., De Leon, G., Thomas, G., Kressel, D., & Peters, J. (1999). The Amity prison TC evaluation: Reincarceration outcome. *Criminal Justice Behavior, 26,* 147–167.

Whitman, J. Q. (2003). *Harsh justice: Criminal punishment and the widening divide between American and Europe.* New York: Oxford University Press.

Wilson, A. B., & Draine, J. (2006). Collaborations between criminal justice and mental health systems for prisoner re-entry. *Psychiatric Services, 57,* 875–878.

Wooden, W. S., & Parker, J. (1982). *Men behind bars: Sexual exploitation in prison.* New York: Plenum.

Wolff, N., & Draine, J. (2004). Dynamics of social capital of prisoners and community re-entry: Ties that bind? *Journal of Correctional Health Care, 10,* 457–490.

World Health Organization (2006). *Tuberculosis in prisons.* Retrieved May 26, 2006 from: http://www.who.int/tb/dots/prisons/story_1/en/.

Inclusion in the Policy Process: An Agenda for Participation of the Marginalized

Margaret Lombe
Michael Sherraden

INTRODUCTION

Modern day polities are built on the principle of exclusion. Examples of these are patriarchal systems and hierarchies built around slavery, racism, sexism, and capitalist systems of production. A number of theories attempt to explain this phenomenon. These include theories of specialization, insider-outsider, and citizenship (Marshall, 1950; Rodgers, 1995; Silver, 1995). During the past few years, under pres-

sure for a more inclusive society brought about by the push for global-
ization and social justice, exclusion has lost its appeal. In fact, in
1995, at the World Summit for Social Development in Copenhagen,
world governments committed themselves to eliminate social exclusion
(UN, 2005). Although headway has been made in this regard through
initiatives advanced by various agencies including the World Bank
(debt relief to highly indebted countries); Global Fund, and World
Health Organization (health promoting initiatives); USAID (focusing
on social development), much more remains to be done to foster
inclusion.

Across nations, poverty has been persistent (International Movement
ATD Fourth World, 1999; United Nations Development Program
(UNDP), 2000; World Bank, 2001). Significant numbers of the world's
citizens cannot even afford basic needs such as food and shelter (FAO,
2005; Serageldin, 1999). In addition, wealth and income inequalities have
risen considerably since the 1980s (Bergesen & Bata, 2002; Schiller,
2003; World Bank, 2001). Within nations, inequality, social, and political
isolation have increased substantially. For example, in the United States
since the 1980s, social isolation and disenfranchisement of the poor and
minority groups has become more marked, more concentrated, and more
firmly implanted in inner city neighborhoods (Wacquant, 1997; Wilson,
1996). Indeed, in the wake of Hurricane Katrina, the world witnessed the
stark inequality and vulnerability of disenfranchised groups in the United
States (the elderly, women, children, and racial minorities). Further, labor
markets, especially in advanced-market economy countries, have become
more fragmented and less stable. Individuals who were once integrated
into mainstream society have been pushed outside the emerging world
system of production (Wacquant, 1997; World Bank, 2001). Moreover,

public disillusionment with government, especially among youth, is on the rise (Harrison & Deicke, 2000; Henn, Weinstein, & Wring, 2002).

Inclusion is likely to remain unattainable for many in the absence of proactive efforts to promote participation of vulnerable individuals and groups. Indeed, building a "society for all" may require deliberate efforts to open up social and political space for vulnerable individuals and groups. One area where this may occur is the policy process. We contribute to the current debate on "inclusive society" by suggesting that inclusion of vulnerable groups in the policy process may be a viable approach toward an inclusive society. This field of inquiry is relative young. Therefore, we first present an overview of the concept of social exclusion/inclusion. We then pinpoint groups at risk of exclusion and underline the extent of their exclusion. Following this, merits of inclusion in the policy process are examined. Functional approaches to inclusion are highlighted. We focus on measurement of inclusion and end with a proposal outlining an agenda for moving forward.

CONCEPTUALIZING SOCIAL EXCLUSION/INCLUSION

The modern discussion of social exclusion/inclusion is strongest in Europe, apparently originating in French Republican rhetoric in the 1960s and 1970s. During that period, social exclusion referred to the shameful and visible condition of people living on the fringe of economic advancement (Lenoir, 1974). This group consisted of traditional marginal groups, e.g., persons with a disability, the mentally handicapped, the aged, the suicidal, and lone parents. The discourse gained prominence in policy and political debates, as well as in academia, during the 1990s with the emergence of the "new poor," referring to persons previously well integrated into mainstream society who had slipped to the margins due to social disadvantage, such as precarious jobs, unemployment, cultural alienation, immigration, weakening of familial networks, and loss of status.

Broadly defined, social exclusion/inclusion is a multidimensional concept delineating a process through which individuals and groups are partially or wholly excluded from or included in participation in their society (Democratic Dialogue, 1995). Social exclusion results from the failure of one or more of four institutions that can integrate individuals and groups into the societal community. These include democratic institutions, which promote civic integration; the labor market, which facilitates economic integration; the welfare state, which promotes social integration; and the family and other social networks, which foster integration into the local community (Bhalla & Lapeyre, 1999; Littlewood & Herkommer, 1999; Rodgers, 1995). The policy process, the focus of the current discussion, is part of democratic institutions.

Extent of Exclusion

Life course analysis has identified groups at risk of exclusion; these include youth, women, single parents, persons with a disability, and older adults (Apospori & Millar, 2003). A common element among persons in these groups is weak or absent attachment to the labor market, which, in an income-driven society, is a major impediment to full social, economic, and political integration. Data from Europe are the best developed and can illustrate the patterns and extent of exclusion for youth, persons with a disability, and the elderly.

Youth

For youth, ages 16 to 29, exclusion is associated with poor educational attainment, lack of skills, precarious jobs, and high unemployment rates. Specific groups, such as youth who leave home at an early age and youth with poor educational qualifications and inadequate skills, are more vulnerable to income poverty and are at greater risk of exclusion (Middleton, 2002). In 2003, youth made up 18 percent of the world's population but 40 percent of the world's unemployed. Within the European Community, in 1995, long-term unemployment rates for youth stood at 50 percent. Currently, the rate of unemployment among youth is about 25 percent. Also, 20 percent of young adults are at risk of poverty even after social transfers (EUROSTAT, 2002; United Nations, 2003).

Persons with a Disability

Exclusion for persons with a disability is closely linked to prejudice and discrimination, limited opportunity, greater likelihood of living alone, inadequate public support, nonrealization of social rights, and other factors that impose barriers to labor force participation (Burchardt, 2000; Heady, 2002). Studies based on the second wave of European Community Household Panel (ECHP) (covering six member countries of the European Union (Austria, Germany, Greece, Norway, Portugal, and United Kingdom) suggest that persons with a disability are more likely to be income poor compared to other adults. Persons in this group are also more likely to suffer material deprivation and more likely to experience social isolation (Heady, 2002). Other studies (e.g., Dupre & Karjalainen, 2003; EUROSTAT, 2002) indicate that adults with a disability are 2.9 times as likely to be outside the formal labor force compared to other adults. Of those employed, 57 percent have low-paying jobs, whereas 42 percent of persons within this group depend on public support for their livelihood.

The Elderly

Among adults aged 65 and older, exclusion is associated with ageism, loss of skills, declining health, weakening social ties, and social isolation. Although income from pensions plays a significant role in preventing poverty among older adults, this group, compared to other adults, is more likely to experience a lack of personal and household necessities. Also, being 75 years and older is associated with declining health and living alone (Middleton, 2002). In fact, 26 percent of older persons living alone are at risk of exclusion (EUROSTAT, 2005).

WHY INCLUSION MATTERS

The concept of inclusion is linked to an ideal of personhood that defines humans, regardless of status, as creative agents endowed with the capacity to influence their life circumstances. Inclusion also places emphasis on "ubuntu"/"cinvivencia"– the interrelatedness of humans. Based on these principles, it is fundamentally unjust and contradictory for vulnerable individuals to be excluded from aspects of citizenship enjoyed by others. A rights perspective (inclusion as a human right) is primary in the discussion of inclusion. Article 1 of the 1948 Universal Declaration of Human Rights acknowledges that all humans are born free and equal in dignity. Human rights are fundamental to building an inclusive society in that they demand full and genuine participation of every citizen in social, political, and economic processes.

Although primary, inclusion-as-a-right is only part of the rationale. Inclusion also matters because (1) it is fundamental to human dignity to participate; (2) exclusion is a cost due to the frayed and torn fabric that holds individuals, households, communities, societies, and polities together;and (3) exclusion reduces capacities of vulnerable persons to realize their potential. In the long term, society pays for this squandered potential in loss of economic productivity and loss of political voice.

Inclusion is the realization that everyone has dignity and everyone has something to contribute. Indeed, vulnerable individuals and groups have a major contribution to make to this discussion; they live the experience of exclusion on a daily basis and, in many respects, they are experts on this subject. Moreover, vulnerable persons must live with consequences of research, interventions, and policy decisions undertaken on their behalf. They should be prominently included in discussions of inclusion. The discussion should move beyond "mainstreaming" to active, positive affirmation of the value and practice of inclusion in all areas, including the policy process.

Why Inclusion in the Policy Process?

In general, mainstreaming has been the central focus of previous efforts to promote social integration (Atkinson & Meulders, 2000; McLennan, 2005). Legislation has been instrumental in laying the foundation for social integration and has created an enabling environment for this to occur. However, legislation has largely been reactive. Legislatures typically lack the political will to engage marginalized groups and give voice to their perspective on issues that affect them (McLennan, 2005). In addition, although regulation has been useful as a mechanism of control, it has not been very effective in creating space for marginalized individuals and groups to participate in mainstream society,nor has it been beneficial in influencing attitudes (Atkinson & Meulders, 2000). Inclusion may require deliberate effort from dominant groups and institutions. This may involve giving up power and control. Inclusion of vulnerable individuals and groups in the policy process is much more than mainstreaming; it complements mainstreaming and extends it further. Inclusion is deliberate effort to proactively engage vulnerable individuals and groups to ensure greater participation. It is based on valued recognition of diversity and solidarity.

Inclusion in the policy process is based on the realization that participation for all, especially the marginalized, matters. The marginalized are not merely recipients of policy and interventions created on their behalf; they are stakeholders and experts on issues that affect them. Inclusion is, therefore, a way to ensure that policy and interventions are responsive to people's felt/expressed needs. Inclusion of vulnerable groups in the policy process sends a message that they matter, they have a stake in society, they have a voice, and the right to be heard. Furthermore, inclusion places an obligation on society, including the marginalized; they begin to feel invested to uphold decisions made with their full participation. Moreover, creating political space guarantees much more than greater community participation; it also reduces disillusionment with government and minimizes feelings of alienation. In a sense, inclusion creates a society of ownership and ensures better social, economic, and political outcomes. Although inclusion of the marginalized in the policy process may be a worthy goal in itself, positive externalities may accrue to the individual, community, and society.

Benefit to the Individual

Benefits to the individual may include the following: feeling part of the process, which entails ownership and obligations; empowerment to influence outcomes, leading to greater orientation to the future; and enhanced dignity and sense of self-worth.

Benefits to the Community

Benefits that may accrue to the community include building legitimacy and trust in the political process; validation of local knowledge by bringing it to the forefront of discussion; and creation of positive externalities, such as stronger social networks, solidarity, cohesion, and interrelatedness.

Benefits to Society

Societal benefits may include creation of communities of stakeholders, development of responsive policies and interventions, building social consensus, and reduction of long-term costs to society by enhancing capacities of marginalized individuals and groups.

Functional Areas

Fundamental to inclusion in the policy process are three functional areas:

1. Participatory methods, which may entail effort/means to engage marginalized individuals and groups;
2. The regulatory framework, which focuses on how formal institutions may be structured to create opportunities for meaningful participation of vulnerable individuals and groups; and
3. Measurement or monitoring, which involves assessment of both process and outcomes. (Carson, 2001,2005)

Much has been written about these functional areas (see e.g., Carson, 2001; Hess, 2005). For this paper we focus on measurement and interventions that may facilitate inclusion. We argue that direct interventions such as institutional constructs deliberately put in place to promote inclusion (e.g., access, information, incentives, expectations, facilitation, and security) and indirect interventions (such as investment in human capital and asset building) may offer useful insights for inclusion in the policy process.

MEASURING INCLUSION AND DATA INADEQUACIES

Measurement of social inclusion is essential in that meaningful interventions are likely to occur only within a framework that measures the concept accurately and consistently. This also enables monitoring and evaluation of policy and program initiatives. At this point, little is known about the meaning of inclusion across countries and cultures generally, or the meaning of inclusion in the policy process specifically. Grounds for inclusion are likely to be different in different cultural contexts; however, effects/outcomes may be similar, e.g., enhanced productivity and consumption capacity, and reduction in rates of poverty, insecurities, and disfranchisement. An important step may be to specify the meanings of inclusion in the policy process, with the goal of acknowledging uniqueness among countries, while looking for constructs that are applicable across countries and cultures for comparative purposes. As mentioned, most theory and data related to inclusion/exclusion are from "developed" countries, predominantly Western Europe. When diverse meanings are better understood, a next important step will be systematic data collection so that a knowledge base can begin to build on a global basis.

Origins of the concept of social exclusion are recent; hence it is not surprising that measures used to assess exclusion are not well developed. The use of social indicators drawn from the three dimensions of participation—economic, political, and social—have been valuable in specifying the nature of exclusion, groups at risk of exclusion, and the extent of exclusion and its correlates. However, this information is not enough. For research to move forward, well-specified indicators that lend themselves to cross-country comparisons should be a priority.

Recent research on social exclusion/inclusion has produced proxy measures for social inclusion in some areas, including income, education, employment, health, housing, and participation in social networks (e.g.,

Bhalla & Lapeyre, 1999; Lombe, 2004; Room, 1995). Despite this headway, the challenge remains the development of a measure of social inclusion that has universal applicability and relevance. The Human Development Index (HDI) and the European Community Household Panel (ECHP) are important steps in this direction.

Measurement of inclusion in the policy process should encompass several aspects and different units of analysis (see Table 1). These may include the following:

1. Laws and regulations designed to promote inclusion, with specific attention to voice and participation by youth, persons with a disability, and the elderly;
2. National level measures of citizen policy involvement, including disbursement of information, participation in civil society groups, participation in political processes, and voting rates;
3. Community level measures of citizen involvement, including disbursement of policy information, participation in community organizations, and role of community-level groups in policy advocacy and policy making;
4. Individual level measures of actual experience in the policy process, including receiving and absorbing information, using information to help guide decisions and actions, and involvement in political processes, either in conjunction with a larger group or individually; and
5. Individual level measures of formal voting, both locally and nationally.

Going forward, the use of such measures in research can include studies at several levels including:

1. Case studies in particular communities, provinces, nations, or regions;
2. Multiple, comparative case studies contrasting levels of inclusion and identifying likely explanations;
3. Large-scale survey assessments within a nation or region;
4. Comparative surveys, such as the Human Development Index, using national level data;
5. Intensive surveys at the individual level;
6. cross-national, comparative surveys at the individual level; and
7. Demonstration research that seeks to test an inclusive strategy against an appropriate counter-factual, in the form of an experiment or quasi-experiment.

TABLE 1. Measurement of inclusion: Unit of analysis and levels at which research can occur

	Individual and Group	Community	National and Cross-national
Unit of Analysis	Individual and Group: May include measures of actual experience of inclusion / exclusion in different dimension, e.g., receiving and absorbing information, using information to help guide decision and actions, and involvement in political processes, access to resources and services, community involvement; participation in the economy, e.g., labor force status, house-hold income, source of household income, and trends of household income	Community: May include community level measures of citizen involvement, including disbursement of policy information, participation in community organizations, and role of community-level-groups in policy advocacy and policy making, as well their role in fostering integration	National and Cross-national: May consist of measures of citizen involvement, including disbursement of information, participation in social, economic and political institutions: Focus ma be on following: 1) Access 2) Information 3) Incentives 4) Expectations 5) Facilitation 6) Security
Nature of Research	Research: This may include intensive surveys both qualitative and quantitative at the individual level; Comparative surveys and cross-national; surveys at the individual level; Demonstration research that seeks to test an inclusive strategy, this could be in the form of an experiment or quasi-experiment	Research: This may focus on case studies in particular communities and provinces within a nation: Multiple, comparative case studies contrasting levels of inclusion and identifying likely explanations for integration or lack of; Demonstration research that seeks to test an inclusive strategy, this could be in the form of an experiment or quasi-experiment	Research: This may include case studies encompassing nations, or regions: large-scale survey assessments within a nation or region: Large-scale survey assessments within a nation or region: Comparative surveys using national level data; Demonstration research that seeks to test an inclusive strategy, this could be in the form of an experiment or quasi-experiment

AGENDA FOR RESEARCH: MIDDLE-RANGE THEORY, DATA COLLECTION, AND ACTION

Direct Interventions: The Role of Middle-Range Approaches

This section is informed by the work coming out of the Center for Social Development (CSD) at Washington University in St. Louis. Scholars at CSD are engaged in programs of applied social research connected to policy, particularly in asset building and civic service. In this work, which occurs in different national and international contexts with a wide range of social conditions, levels of economic development, and political regimes, scholars have begun to focus on levels of study and intervention that can be thought of as "middle range." The perception is that the middle-range approach has greater applicability across different contexts, and is directly relevant in application. The goal is to move beyond idealism to concrete theory and data collection strategies that can specify test, measure, and create successful innovations.

Emphasis is placed on institutions that are purposefully put in place to promote inclusion (e.g., Sherraden, Schreiner, & Beverly, 2003). Although the focus at CSD has been in the areas of asset building and civic service, institutional constructs that have emerged in CSD research may be widely applicable. The following institutional constructs can be used to study and inform innovations for inclusion in the policy process:

1. *access*, meaning eligibility and availability;
2. *information* on the purpose of participation and how to participate;
3. *incentives*, financial or otherwise, to encourage participation;
4. *expectations* for participation, expressed by both leaders and program structures;
5. *facilitation*, meaning concrete assistance with participation; and
6. *security*, meaning safety in participation.

The point of using middle-range thinking and focusing on institutions is that the knowledge generated can have direct policy relevance. For example, in asset building, CSD's work has led to policy and program development in more than 40 U.S. states, the federal government, and several other nations (United Kingdom, Canada, Australia, China, Korea, Peru, and Uganda). This might be one example of building a knowledge base that can directly inform socioeconomic development. A similar process could and should occur with participation in the policy process, and institutional approaches seem equally promising in this context.

Indirect Intervention: The Potential of Education and Asset Building

It could be that some promising ways to promote inclusion in the policy process are not direct, but rather indirect. Especially, it seems likely that primary and secondary education of all members of society leads to greater inclusion in the policy process. Communities with higher investments in human capital enjoy higher social, political, and economic returns compared to communities with low investments in human capital. Evidence also points to enhanced household welfare and civic engagement (Berghman, 1995; Mundle, 1998).

At CSD, research indicates that a saving and asset-building strategy has positive effects on inclusion (Lombe, 2004). Specifically, homeownership and education are linked with all the dimensions of inclusion: economic, political, and social. The likely explanation is that people who own assets have a "stake" in society, and therefore they cognitively pay greater attention and participate more in civic and political activity (Lombe, 2004; McBride, Lombe & Beverly, 2003; Sherraden, 1991). These are only two examples of promising "indirect" strategies to increase inclusion in the policy process. At present, the knowledge base for such strategies is weakly developed, and this may be an important area for future research.

CONCLUSION

The position taken by this article is that inclusion in the policy process is desirable. However, caution should be exercised regarding the fact that conflict may arise between the agenda for inclusion and the choice of "self-exclusion." Some groups, e.g., ethnic minorities may choose, for a variety of reasons to remain outside the mainstream economic, social, and political institutions. Also, such groups may perceive inclusion to be directed at cultural assimilation, suggesting "sameness," threatening identity and group cohesion. Moreover, both the language and agenda for inclusion, as currently articulated, may not be accessible and relevant to the marginalized. When thoughtfully structured, inclusion in the policy process suggests a transformative agenda and points to necessary changes in public policies, attitudes, and institutional practices. Its primary objective extends beyond "bringing people in"; it focuses on ensuring that all people, especially the marginalized, participate as valued members of society.

Creating space for marginalized individuals and groups to participate in the policy process may be a challenging task. However, at a time of great strides in technology, medicine, and human and civil rights, it is ironic that inequality, poverty, and hunger are widespread and thousands of people remain voiceless and excluded from participating in the life of their communities (United Nations, 2005). The profession of social work is uniquely positioned to take the lead in efforts to promote a more inclusive society, a society of greater citizen engagement. Social work has both the mandate and expertise—we work with vulnerable groups on a daily basis; they are our clients. One area of involvement might be to build the capacity of the marginalized so that the opportunity to participate is linked to capabilities. Social workers can advocate for an inclusive regulatory structure, one that facilitates/supports participation of the marginalized. They can also promote participatory processes that are accessible and sensitive to the diverse needs of vulnerable groups.

REFERENCES

Apospori, E., & Millar, J. (2003). *The dynamics of social exclusion in Europe: Comparing Austria, Germany, Greece, Portugal, and the UK.* Cheltonham, UK: Edward Elgar Publishing, Inc.

Atkinson, A., & Meulders, D. (2000). EU action on social inclusion and gender mainstreaming. Economic Research Working Paper.

Bergesen, A., & Bata, M. (2002). Global and income inequality: Are they connected? *Journal of World-Systems Research, 8*(1), 2–6.

Berghman, J. (1995). Social exclusion in Europe: Policy context and analytical framework. In G. Room (Ed.). *Beyond the threshold: The measurement and analysis of social exclusion* (pp. 10–28). Bristol: The Polity Press.

Bhalla, A., & Lapeyre, F. (1999). *Poverty and exclusion in a global world.* London: Macmillan Press.

Burchardt, T. (2000). The dynamics of being disabled. *Journal of Social Policy, 29*(4), 645–668

Carson, L. (2001). Activating the voice of the voiceless, *Third Sector Review, 7*(2), 57–71.

Carson, L. (2005*). Community engagement initiatives in Australia.* Paper presented at the "Towards an inclusive society: Shaping the policy process" workshop, New York, July 13–15.

Democratic Dialogue (1995). *Social exclusion/inclusion.* Special report no. 2. Retrieved June 15, 2001, from http://www.dem-dial.demon.co.uk/index.htm.

Dupre, D., & Karjalainen, A. (2003). Employment of disabled people in Europe. Retrieved June 15, 2005, from http://europa.eu.int/comm/employment_social/health_safety/docs/disabled_.

EUROSTAT (2002). Database. Retrieved June 2005, from http://www.epp.eurostat.cec.eu.int.

EUROSTAT (2005). Database. Retrieved June 2005, from http://www.epp.eurostat.cec.eu.int.

Food and Agriculture Organization of the United Nations (2005). *The state of food insecurity in the world.* United Nations Publication, Sales No. E.05.L.I4.

Harrison, L., & Deicke, W. (2000). Capturing the first time voters: An initial study of political attitude among teenagers, *Youth and Policy, 67*, 26–40.

Heady, C. (2002). Sickness and disability. In M. Barnes, C. Heady, S. Middleton, J. Millar, F. Papadopoulos, et al. (Eds.), *Poverty and social exclusion in Europe* (pp. 101–123). Northampton, UK: Edward Elgar Publishing Inc.

Henn, M, Weinstein, M., & Wring, D. (2002). A generation apart? Youth and political participation in Britain, *British Journal of Politics and International Relations 4*(2), 167–192.

Hess, M. (2005). *Regulatory framework.* Paper presented at the "Towards an inclusive society: Shaping the policy process" workshop, New York, July 13–15.

International Movement ATD Fourth World (1999). *Redefining human rights-based development: The Wresinski approach to partnership with the poor.* Retrieved August 15, 2002, from http://www.atd-quartmonde.org.

Lenoir, R. (1974). *Les Exclus: Un français sur dix.* (Excluded: French on ten). Paris: Seuil.

Littlewood, P., & Herkommer, S. (1999). Identifying social exclusion: Some problems with meaning. In P. Littlewood, I. Glorieux, S. Herkommer, & I. Jonsson, (Eds.), *Social exclusion in Europe: Problems and paradigms* (pp. 1–22). Burlington, Vermont: Ashgate Publishing Company.

Lombe, M. (2004). *Impact of asset ownership on social inclusion.* Doctoral Dissertation, Washington University in St. Louis.

Marshall, T. (1950). *Citizenship and social class and other essays.* Cambridge: Cambridge University Press.

McBride, A., Lombe, M., & Beverly, S. (2003). The effects of Individual Development Account programs: Perceptions of participants. *Social Development Issues, 23*(1/2), 59–73.

McLennan A. (2005). *Challenging the mainstream: Political mechanisms to enhance inclusion.* Paper presented at the "Towards an inclusive society: Shaping the policy process" workshop, New York, July 13–15.

Middleton, S. (2002). Transition from youth to adulthood. In M. Barnes, C. Heady, S. Middleton,J. Millar, F. Papadopoulos, et al.(Eds.), *Poverty and social exclusion in Europe* (pp. 53–79). Northampton, UK: Edward Elgar Publishing Inc.

Mundle, S. (1998). Financing human capital development: Some lessons learned from advanced Asian countries. *World Development, 26*(4), 659–672.

Rodgers, G. (1995). What is special about a social inclusion approach? In G. Rodgers, C. Gore, J. Figueiredo (Eds.), *Social exclusion: Rhetoric, reality, responses* (pp. 43–51). Geneva: International Institute for Labour Studies.

Room, G. (1995). Poverty and social exclusion: The new European agenda for policy and research. In G. Room (Ed.), *Beyond the threshold: The measurement and analysis of social exclusion* (pp. 1–9). Bristol: Policy Press.

Schiller, R. (2003). *The economics of poverty and discrimination* (9th ed.). Englewood Cliffs, NJ: Prentice Hall.

Serageldin, I. (1999). *Poverty and inclusion reflections: A social agenda for the new millennium*. Retrieved July 30, 2002, from http://www.dse.de/ef/poverty/serageldin.htm.

Sherraden, M. (1991). *Assets and the poor: A new American welfare policy*. Armonk, NY: M.E. Sharpe.

Sherraden, M., Schreiner, M., & Beverly, S. (2003). Income and institutions in saving policy. *Economic Development Quarterly, 17*(1), 95–112.

Silver, H. (1995). Reconceptualizing social disadvantage: Three paradigms of social exclusion . In G. Rodgers, C. Gore, J. Figueiredo (Eds.), *Social exclusion: Rhetoric, reality, responses* (pp. 57–77). Geneva: International Institute for Labour Studies.

United Nations Development Program. (2000). *Human development report 2000*. New York: Oxford University Press Inc.

United Nations (2003). Youth Employment. In *World Youth Report 2003: The Global Situation of Young People*, (pp. 54–71). Retrieved July 15, 2005, from http://www. un.org/esa/socdev/unyin/documents/ch02.pdf.

United Nations (2005). *Report on the world social situation: The inequality predicament*. New York: United Nations Publishing Section.

Wacquant, L. (1997). The comparative structure and experience of urban exclusion: Race, class, and space in Chicago and Paris. In K. Mcfate, R. Lawson, & W. Wilson (Eds.), *Poverty, inequality and the future of social policy: Western states in the new world order* (pp. 543–576). New York: Russell Sage Foundation.

Wilson, W. J. (1996). *When work disappears: The world of the new urban poor* (pp.111–145). New York: Alfred A. Knopf.

World Bank (2001). *World Development Report 2000/2001: Attacking poverty*. Oxford University Press.

Service Learning: The Road from the Classroom to Community-Based Macro Intervention

Diane L. Scott

Social work educators must address the needs of social work graduates who face increasingly complex problem situations that require more varied skill competencies to help clients in communities than those taught solely within the field practicum experience (Reisch & Jarman-Rohde, 2000). Social workers must help clients in economically, politically, racially, and ethnically polarized communities to which the workers may not have been exposed in their personal lives and field practice experience. Academicians who fail to adequately prepare students and teach them the requisite skills for changing environments contribute to social worker burnout and a sense of powerlessness (Lager & Cooke Robbins, 2004). Reisch and Jarman-Rohde (2000) strongly suggest that restructuring traditional field placement models, vertical and horizontal integration of content, and expanding opportunities for community-based learning are among the changes needed to adequately prepare social workers for professional practice today.

An integrated service-learning-based curriculum focused on the macro-practice skills needed by social workers in generalist practice can over-come the dichotomy between traditional didactic learning in the classroom and experiential community-based learning. Building upon the social work tradition and value placed upon field practicum learning (Lager & Cooke Robbins, 2004), a direct linkage of learning objectives to service-learning experiences in courses that supplement the traditional field practicum experience helps students integrate micro-, mezzo-, and macro-level skills and apply them to community-based social work practice.

The integrated model presented here directly links social work practice to research and policy, facilitates the integration of course content with relevant social justice issues in the local community, fosters student advo-cacy, interest, and involvement in macro and social policy issues while developing macro–level practice skills, and empowers community groups and disadvantaged populations. This article suggests issues that social work educators face in implementing such an integrated and service–learning–based curriculum model.

SERVICE LEARNING AND SOCIAL WORK FIELD PRACTICE

Service learning has been described as an integrated "credit–bearing educational experience in which students participate in an organized ser-vice activity that meets identified community needs and reflects on the service activity in such a way as to gain further understanding of course content, a broader appreciation of the discipline, and an enhanced sense of civic responsibility" (Bringle & Hatcher, 1996, p. 221).

As does a service–learning perspective, social work education has historically emphasized the importance of the hands–on field learning experience to the development of social work professionals that helps differentiate the social work profession from other professions (Marshack, 1994). Horizontal and vertical integration of social work knowledge, skill development, and practice competency results from the experiential learning that occurs during the practicum experience (Miller, Corcoran, Kavacs, Rosenblum, & Wright, 2005).

Caspi and Reid (1998) emphasize the need for a task–centered model of field instruction that has primary goals of addressing client needs and helping students to obtain social work knowledge and skills. To meet these goals during the field experience, tasks are defined with clear expectations and accountability measures, contain feedback and evaluation processes, and link class and field knowledge.

Linking learning objectives to experiential–based experiences in an agency setting forms the core of the social work field practice experience (Caspi & Reid, 1998; Fortune, Cavazos, & Lee, 2005; Miller et al., 2005). Although not traditionally labeled as such, the field practicum can be viewed as a type of service learning course because the field experience is the capstone experience that integrates the social work knowledge– base, practice skills, critical thinking, and the professional values encompassed within the code of ethics. This is especially true in relation to social workers' responsibility to advocate and promote social justice (NASW, 1999). However, the field placement focus on professional social work skill development differentiates it from the experiential learning that may occur in a service–learning course (Bringle & Hatcher, 1996).

Expanding the service–learning–based courses within the social work curriculum builds upon the traditional internship by providing students with additional exposure to real world problems experienced within communities. Jovanich (2003) identified response to community needs, content integrated to service experiences, and a sustained focus in discussions about civic engagement as the three primary criteria for a service–learning–based course. Rather than engage in solely volunteer work, students intervene in problems identified by agency partners, community groups or grassroots community engagement. Doing so provides them a direct exposure to diverse persons and client situations while giving them an opportunity to actively develop and test –problem solving, negotiation, advocacy, and social justice skills.

CURRICULUM MODEL

Within this model, three social work courses, Human Behavior in Organizations and Communities, Social Policy, and Human Diversity and Social Justice, are linked by curriculum that focuses on active involvement with real social problems within the community rather than scenario–driven role–play exercises (see Figure 1). Students are encouraged to select a social issue in which they have a personal and passionate interest that can be applied across the three courses. Specifically, using existing social problems, students learn how to conduct community assessments, use research–based interventions, conduct policy analysis and evaluation, and plan and carry out community intervention strategies. Thus, students link social problems to micro through macro levels of practice and through their macro–skill development are encouraged to view policy as practice that can be altered by their participation in democratic processes.

To vertically and horizontally integrate content, faculty collaborated to incorporate desired learning outcomes across the three courses (see Figure 2). A primary focus was for students to understand the need to view problems from a broader perspective than solely from that of the individual client. Second, students needed to learn how to assess problems from a larger systems

FIGURE 1. Curriculum model.

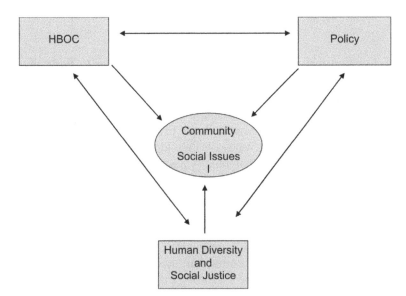

FIGURE 2. Intervention model.

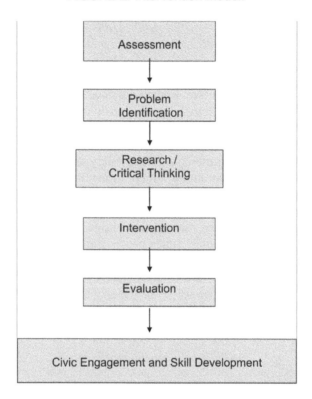

perspective and that the primary skills used were similar to those used in mocro-level practice. Another desired learning outcome was an understanding of power, communication, and group work as important tools for advocacy in the macro arena. Finally, students were to develop mastery of skills to gain confidence in their collective ability to bring about changes in policy and communities, and to develop skills individually so that they would continue their involvement in the community post-graduation.

Human Behavior in Organizations and Communities (HBOC)

Beginning with the foundation course in Human Behavior in Organizations and Communities (HBOC), particular attention is devoted to applying micro and mezzo skills to community assessment to prevent students from imposing solutions before a thorough community needs assessment is completed. Within this curriculum, HBOC is traditionally the first exposure to macro-level content on assessment, but students have prior exposure to social problems and related research. Their enthusiasm and zeal to help people combined with this previous exposure leads to a tendency for students to pick a social problem and solution, then to impose it on a community regardless of need.

To combat the tendency to impose solutions without first assessing need, students are required to conduct a community assessment that forces them to consult census reports and community websites, conduct interviews with influential persons, and learn about the resources available within the community (Kirst-Ashman & Hull, 2006). Particular attention focuses upon the social, political, and economic climate of a community and in identifying persons with power in the different arenas. During the assessment, students are encouraged to begin identifying the social problems that emerge.

Following the community assessment, students select one of the social problems they identified and then review relevant research to find applicable solutions. The overall goal is to develop a program to meet a human service need or to increase community awareness of a social issue or problem. Armed with a solution to address the identified need or issue grounded in research, the students formulate a problem statement, intervention goals, and evaluation measures, and then they begin implementation of a social action campaign.

Social Welfare Policy

The Social Welfare Policy course linkage to HBOC occurs when students select a social issue of interest or current import. Students are required to identify, track, and analyze existing or proposed federal or state legislation. Students are encouraged to choose an issue to analyze that they identified in HBOC. Selecting their community social problem helps students learn that seemingly far-removed decisions that occur at the federal and local levels regarding social policy and funding are actually *local* when implemented to solve a problem in their community. Using applied research and the policy analysis, students evaluate and make policy recommendations to present to legislators.

Unlike most traditional bachelor's-level social welfare policy courses, students learn how to research scholarly journals and navigate government websites to gather information about state and federal legislators, track bills by legislative session and by social issue, and to search for information about state statutes. This reinforces the course content from HBOC in that students are reminded repeatedly of the direct linkage between social problem identification, the political process, research based solutions, and funding streams.

The social welfare policy course diverges into skill development when students use the information and their policy analysis to write drop papers, policy briefs, and letters to legislators. When the legislature is in session, the students take this information directly to the state capitol when they meet in small groups with the legislators in their offices. When not in session, students schedule similar meetings in legislators' local offices. Very concretely, students practice writing and public-speaking skills, learn legislative language, learn the etiquette for legislator access, and most important, get direct experience in advocating with policymakers. Students frequently report being impressed that the legislator took the time to meet with them, but more impressively, *listened* to their presentation of the issues even if it was in opposition to the legislator's publicly stated positions.

Human Diversity and Social Justice

Building upon the macro practice skills the students develop completing their community assessment and research-based solution, and the lobbying work begun in the social welfare policy course, the Human Diversity and Social Justice course (HDSJ) requires students to continue implementation of their action campaign plans. Either individually or in small groups, students connect with local social service agencies or neighborhood groups to implement their plan to improve the status of the policy issue or community problem. The work in HDSJ is designed to give students the opportunity to devote more hours over a longer period with a greater number of community activities from their action campaign plans because the activities span two semesters.

A key component of the community action campaign includes an emphasis on developing measurable objectives directly related to the identified need, ongoing revision and evaluation of the process, and outcome of the change effort. Students may engage in petition-signing efforts, lobby legislators and elected officials, hold public demonstrations, develop letter-writing or media campaigns, or partner with social service agency programs, among other tactics. The following student project illustrates the intertwined content and skill development of this curriculum model.

AIDS Awareness and Prevention Campaign

Three students partnered in the HBOC course to complete their community assessment on Fort Walton Beach, FL. The students gathered information ranging from geographic location to demographics to community livability using the model presented in class (Kirst-Ashman & Hull, 2006). They also interviewed social workers who practice in Fort Walton Beach to determine problem issues. Following the assessment, the students determined that there was a lack of awareness regarding AIDS and its transmission. The local agency serving clients who have AIDS, Okaloosa AIDS Support and Informational Services (OASIS), provided the students information regarding the scope of their current prevention efforts and their service limitations due to funding restraints. The OASIS program had only two paid staff members at the time and relied heavily on volunteers.

In the social welfare policy course, the students then focused their research on the Ryan White Comprehensive AIDS Resources Emergency Act of 1990 (CARE Act), Public Law 101-38, and queried local legislators regarding their positions on funding AIDS programs. The lack of state-level financial support for prevention programs sponsored by OASIS were an impetus for the students' decision to implement an AIDS awareness and prevention project at the university's branch campus in Fort Walton Beach.

The students designed and implemented their project on AIDS prevention in the HDSJ course. They met regularly as a group to plan the event, delegate task assignments, assess progress, and regroup. The project was coordinated with OASIS to hand out educational materials and conduct HIV testing on campus. They met with business and community leaders to disseminate information throughout the Fort Walton Beach area. For the core of their project, the students set up information tables and had HIV testing available on campus on seven separate dates. The three students designed publicity (letters of interest to community agencies, flyers, e-mail announcements, radio ads), secured the informational materials and testing kits from OASIS, and staffed the event. Twenty-four persons were tested on the first date, 3 persons tested on the second date, 17 were tested on the third date; 2 were tested on the fourth date, no one attended the fifth date, 2 were tested on the sixth date; no one attended the seventh; and 3 attended the eighth. The students secured commitment from the university and OASIS to schedule HIV testing monthly through the end of the year. In addition, the students worked with OASIS to meet with local business owners to place flyers and condom baskets in the business locations. The flyers show the schedule of testing dates for the remainder of the year.

SERVICE LEARNING ACTIVITIES

Students who engage in community-based activities connected with the three macro-based courses receive credit for the hours they work from the university service-learning department. For example, students log hours for attending public meetings, interviewing influential stakeholders, working on the community events in their action plan, lobbying legislators, and organizing their action group. Students report from 20 to 100 community-based hours from the three courses combined. Rather than being an unfamiliar requirement, for 70 percent of students (Astin, 1996 as cited in Hinck & Brandell, 2000), community service effort at the university level simply expands upon the community service involvement during high school. To recognize the students' efforts within the community, the university records service learning hours on official transcripts (Volunteer UWF!, n.d.). Students must attain at least 20 hours in the course of the semester to get the hours documented; if students do not log the minimum 20 hours in the course of one semester, the hours roll over into the next semester and may be combined with other service learning activity hours to reach the minimum.

Most important, the students' active participation in the community, and their applied efforts to bring about change based upon course content, reinforce the difference between "volunteering" and service learning. The hands-on, real-world social work experience provides students the opportunity "to make sense of the social world in ways that do not rely on linear logic of textbooks" (Jonavich, 2003, p. 81). Students develop skills in working as part of a team, in leadership positions, in conflict resolution, and in community development while mastering macro-level social work practice. The end result is that they learn to be active participants in democracy that may lead to increased civic engagement upon graduation.

IMPLEMENTATION ISSUES

Use of an integrated curriculum model that incorporates service learning in the community must be supported by faculty members committed to the premise behind service learning, i.e., the community becomes a laboratory for student learning. As such, faculty members must support the premise that service learning is an educational philosophy and an instructional method (Bringle, Games, Foos, Osgood & Osborne, 2000). Similarly, faculty must invest extra time and effort to become familiar with community issues themselves (Abes, Jackson, & Jones, 2002), and to be invested in empowering students to engage in change efforts. Extra time devoted to office hours and meetings in community settings is critical to the success of student efforts. Time constraints, combined with students who live and work in geographic locations far removed from university facilities, demand faculty availability with flexibility in task assignments and measures of student learning. Since community problems and settings are so varied, faculty must decrease their reliance upon testing and assessment measures that focus on classroom-based content to reflective assignments that demonstrate skill-based competencies (Hatcher & Bringle, 1997; Strouse, 2003). A positive outcome for social work faculty members who use a service learning-based approach is that it may reintegrate academicallyfocused social workers with the community and provide them with up-to-date classroom examples.

An implementation issue that may arise for some social work programs, as it does for faculty currently using this model, is the rise in nontraditional students. Students and faculty members using this model must negotiate conflicts in schedules, work and family demands, as well as class schedules when coordinating service-learning activity for a student population that is weighted more toward nontraditional students with family and work responsibilities who reside off-campus as opposed to a traditional campus-based student population.

Although a component of service, the increased demands from a service learning community-based activity are not always recognized in faculty workloads, nor do they count toward tenure and promotion (Hammond, 1994 as cited in Bringle, Hatcher, & Games, 1997). To the contrary, both faculty and the university may be more visible than before the service-learning project because students frequently identify issues that challenge existing norms and the status quo. Depending upon how well the university is positioned in partnership with the local community, increased visibility may be viewed as either a liability or something to be welcomed.

IMPLICATIONS FOR SOCIAL WORK

Within the social work profession, using this service-learning-based curriculum model to develop an affinity for macro-level practice and community involvement may require a philosophical shift in how practice is viewed. This model presumes that macro-based practice is skill based, therefore has a corresponding need to provide students with real-world field experience to foster skill development. Rather than be solely a volunteer experience, the service-learning project must be connected to the content and be viewed as an integral part of the course. As such, service-learning-based courses may appear to be in conflict with or a challenge to existing internship requirements, particularly in programs with a strong micro-practice focus.

In addition to macro-skill development, the service learning experience reinforces the interconnection between policy and social work practice (Influencing State Policy, 2006) and helps students make direct connections between legislation and their local community. Another important effect of incorporating macro service-learning-based curriculum is that it reconnects students with core social work values to promote social justice and engage in advocacy (NASW Code of Ethics, 1999). Similarly, providing students community-based experience expands upon strengths and competency-based models by capitalizing upon the skills students develop in traditional internships and connects them with diverse population groups with whom they may have had no prior exposure, e.g., economically disadvantaged or immigrant groups.

Students emerge from the courses presented herein with a sense that their activities and participation in the community are valued and a necessary part of a democratic society. Service-learning research suggests that the long-term outcome from this involvement as a student is increased civic engagement throughout their lives (Bringle & Hatcher, 1995). Enhancing students' perception of the value of civic engagement to their professional career reinforces the likelihood that students will remain engaged.

REFERENCES

Abes, E. S., Jackson, G., & Jones, S. R. (2002). Factors that motivate and deter faculty use of service-learning. *Michigan Journal of Community Service Learning, 9*(1), 5–17.

Bringle, R. G., Games, R., Foos, C.L., Osgood, R., & Osborne, R. (2000). Faculty fellows program. Enhancing integrated professional development through community service. *American Behavioral Scientist, 43*(5), 882–894.

Bringle, R. G., & Hatcher, J. A. (1995). A service-learning curriculum for faculty. *Michigan Journal of Community Service Learning, 2,* 112–122.

Bringle, R. G., & Hatcher, J. A. (1996). Implementing service learning in higher education. *The Journal of Higher Education, 67(2),* 221–239.

Bringle, R.G., Hatcher, J.A., & Games R. (1997). Engaging and supporting faculty in service learning. *Journal of Public Service and Outreach, 2*(1), 43–51.

Caspi, J., & Reid, W. J. (1998). The task-centered model for field instruction: An innovative approach. *Journal of Social Work Education, 34*(1), 55–70.

Fortune, A. E., Cavazos, A., & Lee, M. (2005) Field education in social work: Achievement motivation and outcome in social work field education. *Journal of Social Work Education, 41*(1), 115–129.

Hatcher, J. A., & Bringle, R. G. (1997). Reflection: Bridging the gap between service and learning. *College Teaching, 45*(4), 153–158.

Hinck, S. S., & Brandell, M. E. (2000). The relationship between institutional support and campus acceptance of academic service learning. *American Behavioral Scientist, 43*(5), 868–881.

Influencing State Policy. (May 7, 2006). Retrieved October 30, 2006, from http://www.statepolicy.org/about_us/purpose.html.

Jovanich, S. (2003). Communication as critical inquiry in servicelearning. *Academic Exchange, 7*(2), 81–85.

Kirst-Ashman, K. K., & Hull, G. H. (2006). *Generalist practice with organizations and communities* (3rd ed.). Belmont, CA: Brooks/Cole Social Work.

Lager, P. B., & Cooke Robbins, V. (2004). Field education: Exploring the future, expanding the vision (Guest Editorial). *Journal of Social Work Education, 40*(1), 3–12.

Marshack, E. (1994). Section IV: Social work education. In S. Hoberman, & S. Mailick (Eds.), *Professional education in the United States. Experiential learning, issues,and prospects* (pp. 103–122). Westport, CT: Praeger, Publishers.

Miller, J., Corcoran, J., Kovacs, P. J., Rosenblum, A., & Wright, L. (2005). Field education: Student and field instructor perceptions of the learning process. *Journal of Social Work Education, 41*(1), 131–145.

National Association of Social Workers (NASW). (1999). *Code of ethics (revised).* Washington, DC: Author.

Reisch, M., & Jarman-Rohde, L. (2000). The field of social work in the United States: Implications for field education. *Journal of Social Work Education, 36*(2), 201–214.

Strouse, J. H. (2003). Reflection as a service-learning assessment strategy. *Journal of Higher Education Outreach and Engagement, 8*(2), 75–88.

Volunteer, UWF! (n.d.). Retrieved October 10, 2006, from http://uwf.edu/volunteer/

Teaching Students to Become Effective in Policy Practice: Integrating Social Capital into Social Work Education and Practice

Robin L. Ersing
Diane N. Loeffler

INTRODUCTION

In recent years, social capital has become widely accepted as an integral part of an effective poverty alleviation strategy and has been used to enhance social justice (Estes, 2003; Warren, Thompson & Saegert, 2002; Woolcock, 2000; World Bank, 2003). In light of this, social workers must integrate social capital more fully into social work policy practice. In order to do so, social work educators must recognize the complexities of social capital and must provide opportunities for students to learn about the utility of social capital within policy and practice realms. Since its inception, professional social work has used elements of social capital in interventions at the micro, mezzo, and macro levels. However, seldom are these interventions discussed in terms of social capital. If "people with good access to social capital tend to be more hired, housed, healthy and happy than those without" (Australian Productivity Commission, 2003, p. xi) then we must ensure that professional social workers understand and effectively use social capital in policy practice.

As social workers, our commitment to social justice requires that we embrace, understand, and use social capital to help overcome the widening inequitable social distribution of resources that continues to exclude many individuals, families, communities, and even nations from accessing opportunities and resources. This begins with teaching our students how to create and maximize social capital when advocating for policy change at local, state, national, and international levels.

Changes in social work practice begin with changes in social work education. As Healy and Hampshire (2003) remind us, "social capital is an important concept in public policy and debate and so it is vital that social workers have an understanding of its origins and implications" (p. 236). By providing our students with an understanding of social work's historical relationship to social capital and by creating opportunities for our students to learn about social capital through experiences, we will enhance our ability, as a profession, to contribute to the growing body of knowledge related to social capital and to more fully participate in effective policy practice.

This article provides a brief definition and overview of social capital using the Loeffler, et al. (2004) framework to integrate social capital and social work practice. We then focus on how social work educators can further students' abilities to utilize social capital in policy practice to enhance social justice.

DEFINING SOCIAL CAPITAL

Social capital can be understood as an empowering process that promotes the building of trusting relationships across individuals, families, and communities to accumulate concrete resources aimed at improving one's quality of life and well-being. The deployment or leveraging of accumulated "capital" (i.e., the level of strength and trust inherent to the social relationships formed), reveals the value of the process according to the types and utility of resources obtained. Examples of such resources acquired through the social capital process of building strong relational ties might include access to new forms of knowledge and information, access to previously constrained economic opportunities, and the use of skills to cultivate additional new forms of financial and/or political capital. Capital typically refers to tangible things. Social capital, in contrast, is a *process*. Therefore, social capital generates access to other forms of capital. Trust, reciprocity, networks, social agency and shared norms all increase/enhance the development of social capital (Estes, 2003; Frank & Yasumoto, 1998; Lin, Cook, & Burt, 2001; Loeffler et al., 2004).

Social capital has a rich theoretical and conceptual history that is beyond the scope of the current discussion (see Farr, 2004 and Woolcock, 1998), Rather, we focus on introducing elements of social capital that will allow educators to integrate social capital into the curriculum. Social capital is often delineated into three interrelated areas: bonding, bridging, and linking. These are closely aligned with the micro, mezzo, and macro areas of practice that are familiar within the generalist framework for social work education and practice (Loeffler et al., 2004). In discussing these interrelated areas, we assume interconnectedness and reciprocity among the three. Indeed, we contend that social capital is integral in accessing resources that are otherwise unavailable given structural and political barriers that block access to resources. Although multilayered, social capital can ultimately create and harness opportunities for connectivity, trust, reciprocity, and mutual benefit for individuals, families, and communities.

Bonding, Bridging, and Linking

For a complete overview of how the social capital concepts of bonding, bridging, and linking are aligned with the micro, mezzo, and macro areas of social work practice, we refer the reader to Loeffler et al. 2004. However, a brief mention of the terms provides context for this discussion of social capital, social work education and policy practice.

Bonding social capital exists within the individual's capabilities to harness the resources that exist/occur within a given relationship. Interpersonal interactions that generate mutual trust, understanding, reciprocity, and shared norms are the building blocks of bonding social capital (Loeffler et al., 2004).

Bridging social capital connects formal and informal support networks. Involvement in faith communities, self-help organizations, and connection with professional peers can all help to generate bridges that provide access to resources such as physical, financial, political, or human capital. Oftentimes, bridging extends relationships across communities (Loeffler et al., 2004).

From a macro perspective, linking social capital focuses on accessing resources and capital from government agencies such as welfare agencies or housing authorities (Woolcock, 2000), access to local, state, and national politicians, and to public policy development. In creating linkages, social work professionals become engaged in social welfare policy and help in the improvement of access to and reallocation of resources and capital. (Loeffler et al., 2004).

Educating our future social work practitioners and policymakers about the interconnectedness between bonding, bridging, and linking social capital is warranted. Indeed, educating them about the interconnectedness between social capital and other forms of capital important in poverty alleviation (economic, financial, human, and cultural capital), is also necessary. The result is an opportunity to reframe discussions of oppression and injustice, creating new and viable solutions for the challenges that face social work practitioners in the twenty-first century.

SOCIAL WORK AND SOCIAL CAPITAL

The social work profession has a long history of embracing social capital as a core element in working with individuals, groups, and communities, though we rarely refer to what we are doing as "building social capital." Indeed, from the earliest days of the Settlement House Movement through the turbulent times of the War on Poverty, the building and strengthening of social ties within families and communities has been central to addressing issues of social justice and social reform (Carson, 1990; Elshtain, 2002; Fisher, 1994; Weil, 1996).

In the past two decades, however, the connection between social work and social capital has become less evident. The growing trend toward clinical social work practice has left many social workers without necessary knowledge and tools to purposefully engage in policy practice, including the development and preservation of social capital. The Alliance for Children and Families (ACF) found that community-based agencies have trouble recruiting social workers to fill jobs in community-centered programs. Further, their study revealed that organizations interested in community practice have continually looked outside of social work to fill their employment gaps. Clergy and other professionals without social work education/credentials have been recruited to step into positions with community-based organizations that have traditionally been "social work jobs" (Ryan, DeMasi, Heinz, Jacobson, & Ohmer, 2000, p. 8). This is particularly noteworthy in the current century when the politics of "new federalism" and devolution have forced communities and individuals to redress socioeconomic disparities plaguing some of our most vulnerable populations who live in low-income communities across the nation.

Without the "social work" focus on community and coalition building, many of these communities and vulnerable populations face eroding social capital and increased alienation. The devolution of federal social welfare policies has shifted responsibility for the care of vulnerable populations to communities and individuals. Thus, individuals are more often reliant upon the support found within formal and informal community-based networks, including faith communities and extended family groups, pooling resources to attempt to mutually build their capacity to overcome these barriers to opportunity (Anderson & Eamon, 2004; Coulton, 1996, 2003; Newman, 1999). Whereas social capital helps to keep individuals and communities "hired, housed, healthy and happy . . . a lack of social capital may encumber daily life, limit social and economic opportunities, and cause markets to work less efficiently. Low social capital in depressed communities can reinforce existing inequalities" (Australian Productivity Commission, 2003, p. xi).

Embracing social capital and integrating it into our educational curricula will be of benefit to the profession—and the populations we serve—as we continue to struggle with the complexities and many faces of poverty and injustice in the twenty-first century. Further, social capital is being incorporated into social work education in other countries and, in a "shrinking world," it is imperative that our students are aware of the concept and its utility both here and abroad. Duncan (1999) poignantly illustrates the impact of persistent class inequalities and weak economies that create little opportunity for moving out of poverty. Restricted opportunity to access capital *can* be overcome through the creation, maintenance, and use of social capital. Low-income children and families are often tied to poor schools and other marginalized resources, which decrease access to opportunities that would "support their efforts to move beyond poverty" (Harris & Zimmerman, 2003, p. 5).

POLICY PRACTICE AND SOCIAL CAPITAL

As social workers, we are charged with challenging social injustices through social change efforts (NASW, 1999). Further, we are charged with "ensur[ing] access to needed information, services, and resources; equality of opportunity; and meaningful participation in the decision making for all people" (NASW, 1999, p. 5). By creating opportunities for oppressed and vulnerable populations to have a voice in the policy process, we begin to challenge policies and programs made in the absence of input from those most impacted by the programs and policies. Social workers can serve as the conduit that links populations and people to policymakers and to the decision-making process. By using our skills as advocates and organizers, we can empower vulnerable populations to have a voice in the policy-making process.

Too often, the elite make decisions that impact marginalized individuals and vulnerable communities in the absence of those who will be affected by policies, programs, and funding cuts. When marginalized populations have a voice in the decision-making processes that yield capital and access to power—or to those with power—and are able to create an opportunity for their needs to be met, they become effective agents of change within both their own household and the broader community. In creating linkages, social work professionals become engaged in social welfare policy and help in the improvement of access to and reallocation of resources and capital (Loeffler et al., 2004).

Social workers must be able to harness the potential of social capital to help build and re-build necessary social networks, programs, and financial resources to maintain programs that benefit the vulnerable populations with whom we work. At the micro, mezzo, and macro levels of social work practice, there are opportunities for social workers to engage in the development and maintenance of bonding, bridging, and linking social capital. This capital, in turn, helps to create or further opportunities and access to resources and power for individuals, families, and communities. Too often policy practice becomes an adjunct to a social worker's "primary" job responsibility. For example, a social worker engaged in supporting victims of domestic violence may engage in day-to-day work as a broker, a counselor, and an educator, yet may also need to work on a broader level as an advocate and an agent of social change. A clinical social worker may engage primarily in counseling and related work but may also spend time working to lobby for parity in insurance coverage for mental health services. If each of these social workers were, as students, given an opportunity to understand how social capital can enhance policy practice, they would be better equipped to work toward advancing institutional and systemic change as well.

It is imperative that as educators we reintroduce our students to the powerful role that social capital can play in the development of social policy and in the fight for reallocation of resources and social justice. In doing so, we may also begin to revitalize students' interest in policy practice as more than an adjunct responsibility.

INTEGRATING SOCIAL CAPITAL AND SOCIAL WORK EDUCATION

Teaching students about the concept, process, and utility of social capital in capacity building and creating social justice presents an exciting opportunity for social work educators. We already create opportunities for students to learn through traditional paths in social work educationby focusing primarily on imparting knowledge, values, and skills necessary for effective work with client systems. This generally entails the use of dynamic role-plays and reflection on field practicum experiences to critically assess the application of skills used to enhance client functioning or to demonstrate the use of problem-solving processes to aid in managing a client situation. Through these experiences, students acquire necessary problem solving, interpersonal and communication skills that can assist them in all aspects of their professional lives.

To complement this education, we must think "outside of the box," taking students down a second path, one that holds the most promise for truly teaching about the power and utility of social capital in pursuit of social justice. In order to do this, we must first engage students in the process of developing their own social capital by providing opportunities for bridging and linking as they prepare to enter the realm of professional social work practice. Second, we must promote learning opportunities that enable students to see first-hand how vulnerable and marginalized individuals and communities can benefit from enhanced social capital.

By facilitating the development of professional relationship building and networking (assisting students in developing their own social capital), we can help our students become more effective in their helping role with clients. Livermore and Neustrom (2003) found that social workers were reliant upon their own social capital in aiding TANF recipients in securing employment—illustrating the need for social work students to begin to develop the trusting relationships and norms of reciprocity that can be useful professionally. Ultimately, by helping students to engage in relationship building and networking, we assist them in understanding the ways that social capital can be leveraged to garner necessary resources to achieve their goals as helping professionals. Students begin to understand how social work professionals can increase their effectiveness in carrying out the role of broker if they have been successful in bonding with more experienced co-workers thus benefitting from their knowledge. Likewise, students who use their social capital developed through networking relationships are able to bridge with colleagues in other organizations to obtain services needed by a client system. This path of learning is a particularly important component for preparing students to become effective in policy advocacy efforts.

Assisting students in understanding the concept of social capital is a vital element in engaging in macro-level change. Students begin to learn the importance of linking mobilized communities with external institutions to pursue structural changes through policy initiatives and influencing decision makers. This experience will aid students in becoming more proficient in their future advocacy efforts to benefit clients and the profession.

Incorporating theoretical, historical, and practical knowledge about social capital helps to transcend the longstanding myth of the micro-macro dichotomy in professional social work practice. Instead, students will learn about social work's distinct approach to addressing social injustices, problems in daily living, and conditions that interfere with healthy human relationships through interventions at the individual, family, organizational, community, and societal levels. The process of social capital spans each level of intervention with the concepts of bonding (micro), bridging (mezzo), and linking (macro). Students should receive guidance in connecting the bonding process of social capital to micro-level practice that involves nurturing social ties within the family system (Coleman, 1988). At the mezzo level of practice, students can be taught about the mobilization of community-based resources and the building of strong social ties with neighbors and local organizations to enhance individual and family well-being (Altschuler, Somkin, & Adler, 2004). Similarly, lessons learned about the role of social capital at the macro level will involve the concept of harnessing collective efficacy within communities and linking them to external institutions that engage in policy making.

Educators can draw from models of locality development, neighborhood and community organizing, and social and economic development to teach fundamental skills and worker roles (Rothman, 2001; Weil & Gamble, 1995). This will help students recognize the strength of social capital and relationships in removing barriers to opportunity structures to achieve justice through the equitable distribution of resources in our society.

Integrating a social capital perspective into policy and practice courses that teach about the often overlooked yet critical mezzo level of intervention serves an important dual purpose in preparing students as social workers. Here students come to understand the pivotal role workers play in successfully bridging the gaps between family or group needs, and the supports and resources available within the broader social and physical environment. Whether connecting families to school systems or grieving parents to mutual support groups, bridging social capital becomes central to mezzo-level work.

A second learning opportunity for social work students focuses on professional development and the need to acquire a personal cache of social capital. This asset can then be applied toward increasing effectiveness in traditional social work bridging roles (e.g., broker, facilitator, and organizer). The field setting is a prime context for educators to encourage students in building professional relationships with formal and informal supports throughout the community. Therefore we recognize that the same principles of trust and reciprocity become vital to professional success in alleviating social injustices that impact our client systems.

An interesting phenomenon often overlooked by faculty and administrators is the fact that students seem to employ social capital as a bridging strategy as they form study circles or project groups. In this regard, the development of social ties and trusting relationships serves as a natural support among peers hoping to achieve a greater success in the program. Likewise, instructors can encourage the building and bridging of social capital between students and formal institutions or informal associations by creating assignments that require interactions with these entities outside the classroom setting (e.g., service learning projects, participatory action research). For some, this subtle approach might suggest a culture shift on the part of administrators and faculty.

Although we teach our students how to use social capital in their work with clients to build both individual and community capacity, we must be cognizant of the need to help students cultivate their own social capital resources as well. In doing so, it is helpful to think about bonding, bridging, and linking social capital as related to students' own self-efficacy, networking, and social justice, respectively. As students enhance their own skills, they will be better prepared to help client systems create, nurture, and sustain social capital that will enable positive social change. Likewise, the forethought by schools of social work to infuse a social capital perspective into the curriculum can reap additional benefits as students forge strong ties and links with the institution manifested through future roles as adjunct instructors, field educators, and recruitment ambassadors.

As educators, we help students create their own interpersonal relationships with their cohort and with –mentors, creating trusting, reciprocal relationships that can be used as a resource in practice (bonding). We create bridges for students so they can understand and access resources and services in the community, and we help students become advocates for social justice, providing linkages with government and institutions, providing platforms and opportunities for change. By creating opportunities for engaged learning, social work educators are able to transform policy and practice knowledge from the curriculum into active applications beyond the walls of the classroom. Opportunities such as interfacing with the state political process and creating social change in a low-income neighborhood, help students see firsthand the power of social capital while providing outlets and opportunities for personal capacity building, relationship building, and resource building. These skills will enable students to work more effectively within their own communities as professional social workers.

CONCLUSION

For social workers to remain involved in policy practice, we must acknowledge that the integration of social capital into community development and poverty alleviation is being used all around us and we must contribute to the knowledge and discussion related to social capital's viability as part of a social justice oriented antipoverty strategy. Social capital is already an integral part of international antipoverty efforts (Estes, 2003; Warren, Thompson & Saegert, 2002; Woolcock, 2000; World Bank, 2003) and social work needs to remain participatory in discussions and interventions that utilize social capital as we can offer a unique perspective related to the complexities of the interface between the individual (or family) and the community. Within social work, social capital is generating interest. Recent works by Fram (2004), Dominguez and Watkins (2003), Coulton (2003), Livermore and Neustrom (2003) and Schneider (2002, 2006) discuss social capital as it relates to social work practice.

Schneider (2006) highlights the importance of social capital in the success of "welfare to work" programs, stressing that former welfare recipients often find jobs and opportunities because of their social capital. Further, she stresses that social welfare policies cannot work in an era of devolution unless formal connections exist between government agencies, private nonprofit organizations, and for-profit organizations. Walker (2004) discusses social capital in the role of social welfare policy and policy analysis in New Zealand, calling for "increased relationship building and networking between agencies—in an era of budget cuts and stretched resources" (p. 4). These examples suggest that social work is starting to embrace social capital, understanding its integral role in creating and maintaining effective social welfare policies and practices. As educators, we must now make the integration of social capital mainstream.

The concept of social capital and its relevance to social work policy practice continues to emerge through academic and scholarly outlets including textbooks (see Bruggeman, 2006; Karger & Stoesz, 2002; Schneider, 2006). Although several curriculum areas are ripe for infusing content on social capital, this article has focused on the infusion of social capital into the policy curriculum, emphasizing the ability of social capital to help create social change and to alleviate injustices and the inequitable distribution of resources and power. As social work educators, we must continue to work for social justice, and this can start by creating opportunities for teaching about social capital in the classroom and beyond. By doing so, we can help to reinforce social work's commitment to social justice and, in turn, will help our students to become responsible practitioners who work to achieve greater equity in an unequal society through effective policy practice and advocacy.

REFERENCES

Altschuler, A., Somkin, C. P., & Adler, N. E. (2004). Local services and amenities, neighborhood social capital, and health. *Social Science and Medicine, 59,* 1219–1229.
Anderson, S. G., & Eamon, M. K. (2004). Health coverage instability for mothers in working families. *Social Work, 49*(3), 395–406.

Australian Productivity Commission. (2003). Social capital: Reviewing the concept and its policy implications. Melbourne, Victoria, AU: Author. Retrieved June 2007 from http://www.pc.gov.au/research/commres/socialcapital/socialcapital.pdf.

Bruggeman, W. G. (2006). *The practice of macro social work* (3rd ed.). Belmont, CA: Thomson/BrooksCole.

Carson, M. (1990). *Settlement folk: Social thought and the American settlement movement, 1885–1930.* Chicago: University of Chicago Press.

Coleman, J. S. (1988). Social capital in the creation of human capital. *American Journal of Sociology, 94* (Supplement), S95–S120.

Coulton, C. J. (1996). Poverty, work and community: A research agenda for an era of diminishing federal responsibility. *Social Work, 41*(5), 509–520.

Coulton, C. J. (2003). Metropolitan inequities and the ecology of work: Implications for welfare reform. *Social Service Review, 77*(2), 159–192.

Domínguez, S., & Watkins, C. (2003). Creating networks for survival and mobility: social capital among African-American and Latin-American low-income mothers. *Social Problems 50*(1), 111–135.

Duncan, C. (1999). *Worlds apart: Why poverty persists in rural America.* New Haven, CT: Yale University Press.

Elshtain, J. B. (2002). *The Jane Addams reader.* New York: Basic Books.

Estes, R. (2003, April 15). *Social capital: A new concept or old wine in new bottles?* Paper presented at the University of Kentucky, College of Social Work, Lexington, KY.

Farr, J. (2004). Social capital: A conceptual history. *Political Theory, 32* (1), 6–33.

Fisher, R. (1994). *Let the people decide: Neighborhood organizing in America.* New York: Twayne Publishers.

Fram, M. S. (2004). Research for progressive change: Bourdieu and social work. *Social Service Review* (December 2004), 553–576.

Frank, K., & Yasumoto, J. (1998). Linking action to social structure within a system: Social capital within and between subgroups. *American Journal of Sociology, 104*(3), 642–686.

Harris, R., & Zimmerman, J. (2003, November). *Children and poverty in the rural south.* Southern Rural Development Center Policy Series, *2*, 1–7.

Healy, K., & Hampshire, A. (2003). Social capital: A useful concept for social work? Australian Social Work, *55*(3), 227–239.

Karger, H. J. & Stoesz, D. (2002). *American social welfare policy: A pluralist approach* (4th ed.). Boston: Allyn & Bacon.

Lin, N., Cook, R., Burt, R., Eds. (2001). *Social capital: Theory and research.* New York: Aldine de Gruyter.

Livermore, M., & Neustrom, A. (2003). Linking welfare clients to jobs: Discretionary use of worker social capital. *Journal of Sociology and Social Welfare, 30* (2), 87–103.

Loeffler, D. N., Christiansen, D., Tracy, M., Secret, M., Ersing, R. L., Fairchild, S., et al. (2004). Social capital for social work: Towards a definition and conceptual framework. *Social Development Issues, 26*(2/3), 22–38.

NASW (1999). *Code of ethics of the National Association of Social Workers.* Washington, DC: NASW.

Newman, K. (1999). *No shame in my game: The working poor in the inner city.* New York: Alfred Knopf.

Rothman, J. (2001). Approaches to community intervention. In J. Rothman, J. Ehrlich, & J. Tropman (Eds.), *Strategies of community intervention* (6th ed.) (pp. 27–64). Itasca, IL: F. E. Peacock.

Ryan, W. P., DeMasi, K., Heinz, P. A., Jacobson, W., & Ohmer, M. (2000, July). Aligning education and practice: Challenges and opportunities in social work education for community-centered practice. Washington, DC: Alliance for Children and Families. Retrieved November 14, 2004, from http://www.alliance1.org/Publications/Aligning.pdf.

Schneider, J. (2002). Social capital and community supports for low-income families: Examples from Pennsylvania and Wisconsin. *The Social Policy Journal, 1*(1), 35–55.

Schneider, J. (2006). Social capital and welfare reform: Organizations, congregations, and communities. New York: Columbia University Press.

Walker, A. (2004). Understanding social capital within community/government policy networks. *Social Policy Journal of New Zealand, 22*, 1–18.

Warren, M. R., Thompson, J. P., & Saegert, S. (2002). The role of social capital in combating poverty. In S. Saegert, J. P. Thompson, & M. R. Warren (Eds.), *Social capital and poor communities* (pp. 1–28). New York: Russell Sage.

Weil, M. (1996). Moral development in community practice: A historical perspective. *Journal of Community Practice, 3* (3/4), 5–67.

Weil, M., & Gamble, D.N. (1995). Community practice models. In *The Encyclopedia of Social Work* (19th ed.) (pp. 577–593). Washington, DC: NASW Press.

World Bank. (2003). *Social Capital.* Retrieved September 23, 2003, from http://www.worldbank.org/poverty/scapital/whatsc.htm.

Woolcock, M. (1998). Social capital and economic development: Toward a theoretical synthesis and policy framework. *Theory and Society, 27*(2), 151–208.

Woolcock, M. (2000). Friends in high places? An overview of social capital. *Id21 insights.* Retrieved October 12, 2003, fromhttp://www.id21.org/insights/insights34/insights-iss34-art02.html.

Index

abortion 70-1, 76-7, 81, 84
ACORN (Association of Community
  Organization Organizations for Reform
  Now) 36, 37-8, 45
activist movements
    advocacy 53
    behaviour change model
      46-8
    commitment 53
    direct services 32-49
    feminist organizations 35-6
    literature review 34-6
    living wage movement, case study
      on 33-49
    locality development model 35-6
    models 35-6, 46-8
    social action model 35-6
    social planning policy model 35-6
    Stages of Change Model 46-8
    welfare reform 34-5
advocacy see also electronic advocacy
    Charity Organization Society 52
    executive, influencing the 67-8
    historical perspectives 52-3, 65-6
    Influencing State Policy (ISP) 67
    lobbying 67
    National Association of Social Workers
      (NASW) 66
    policy change, targeting 67-8
    Policy Conference and Policy Practice
      Forum 67
    Progressive era 66
    Settlement House Movement 52
    skills for advocacy 53

social activism, commitment to 53
social capital 143
social work education 66-7
affirmative action 81-2, 84
AIDS awareness and prevention campaign
  131
Alito, Samuel 69-70, 71-84
asset building, social inclusion and 120
assisted suicide, use of controlled drugs in
  75

behaviour change model 46-8
blogs 57
bonding, bridging and linking 138-9, 141-4

campaigns, limits to contributions to and
  expenditure on 76
capital see social capital
capital punishment 77-8, 79
Centre for Social Development (CSD),
  Washington University 119-20
Chafee Act 24-5
Charity Organization Society 52
church and state, separation of 72-3, 78
citizenship, prisoners' barriers to full 98
civil rights in the Supreme Court 70-2,
  77-8, 81-2
collective action 12
community action programs 130
community-based activities 132-3
community needs assessments 128-9
corporations, role of 10-11
Council of Social Work Education
  (CSWE) 46

crime *see also* prisoners
    death penalty 77-8, 79
    defendants and prisoners, rights
      of 70-2, 77
    duress 74
    sentencing, public discourse on 88-90,
      101-2

database management 59
death penalty 77-8, 79
deportation, immigration and 81
digital divide 61-2
disabilities, persons with
    children, individual education programs
      (IEP) for 73, 83
    social exclusion/inclusion 112-13
discrimination 72, 73-4, 76-7, 82-3
drugs 75, 92-3, 97-8, 102-3

economics, social justice through 4-6,
  9-13
    collective action 12
    corporations, role of 10-11
    democratic capitalism 9
    employment policies 10
    health care, proposal for national
      system of 10
    lobbying 12
    minimum wage, raising the 10
    pensions 10
    politics 5-6, 14
education *see also* social work education
  disabled children, individual education
  programs (IEP) for 73, 83
    Educational and Training Voucher
      Programs (ETVPs) 25
    school desegregation and affirmative
      action 81-2, 84
    social exclusion/inclusion 120
elderly 113
elections *see also* electoral politics, social
  justice through 4-14
    campaigns, limits to contributions to
      and expenditure on 76
    explicit advocacy and issue
      advocacy 80
electoral politics, social justice through
  4-14
    changes needed 7-9

collective action 12
conservative domination 5-6
economic policy 5-6, 14
felons, re-enfranchisement of
  6, 8-9
government, role of 5
inequality 5-7, 13
Inequality and American Democracy.
  APSA 6-7, 13
participation, lack of 6-9, 13-14
parties, need for more political 7, 8
proportional representation 8
reform movement, creation of broad 9
electronic advocacy 50-64
  digital divide 61-2
  emergent form of practice, as 54
  non-profit organizations 50-1, 54-6, 62
  resistance 53, 54, 62-3
  Smart Mobs 67
  social or free software 50-1, 54-62
  social work education 54-6, 62-3
  YouTube 61
electronic mailing lists 57-8
email, free 57
employment 10, 72, 73-4, 77, 82-3, 97-9
  see also living wage movement, case
  study on
exclusion *see* social exclusion/inclusion
executive, influencing the 67-8

Facebook 60
field practice 125-6
financial management 59
Flickr 58
free or social software 50-1, 54-62
freedom of speech 74-5, 76, 78, 79-80

Geographical Information Systems (GIS)
  mapping 55
Google Maps 55, 60
Googledocs 59
graphics editing tools 59
Guantanamo Bay, military commissions at
  75-6

health 10, 94-5, 103, 131
housing for ex-prisoners 97, 98, 101
Human Behaviour in Organizations and
  Communities (HBOC) 127, 128-9, 131

Human Diversity and Social Justice
  (HDSJ) 127, 130-1
human rights 113

immigration, deportation and 81
inclusion *see* social exclusion/inclusion
Influencing State Policy (ISP) 67
International Federation of Social Workers
  (IFSW) 46

labour unions 39-40, 44
language 18, 22
learning objectives to experiential-based
  experiences, linking 126
Listserv 57-8
living wage movement, case study
  on 33-49
  ACORN (Association of Community
    Organization Organizations for
    Reform Now) 36, 37-8, 45
  business leaders, threats from 40-3
  Council of Social Work Education
    (CSWE) 46
  endorsements 39-43
  funds 44-6
  government workers 33
  indirect involvement 42-3
  individual and agency support 42-3
  International Federation of Social
    Workers (IFSW) 46
  labour unions 39-40, 44
  lack of support, reasons for 43-6
  methodology 36-9
  National Association of Social Workers
    (NASW) Code of Ethics 46
  neutrality 40
  opposition 40-1
  ordinances 33-4, 38-43
  participant observation 36-7
  political organizing, funds threatened
    by 45-6
  postcard method of gathering
    information 42
  poverty 33
  recruitment 42
  results 39
  social services agencies and
    professionals 33-4
  supporters 36

lobbying 12, 67
locality development model 35-6

mapping tools 55, 60
marginalization *see* social exclusion/
  inclusion
minorities, disproportionate representation
  in prison of 91-2, 99-100
MySpace 60

National Association of Social Workers
  (NASW)
  advocacy 66
  Code of Ethics 46, 66
  living wage movement, case study
    on 46
  Political Action for Candidate Election
    (PACE) 66
  strength-based framework for social
    policy 16-17
  Supreme Court 70-1
newsgroups 58

O'Connor, Sandra Day 68-70
OpenOffice 58-9

participation in electoral politics 8-9,
  13-14
pensions 10
photo journalism online 58
politics
  campaigns, limits to contributions to
    and expenditure on 76
  explicit advocacy and issue advocacy
    80
  living wage movement, case study on
    45-6
  participation, lack of 6-9, 13-14
  parties, need for more political 7, 8
  Political Action for Candidate Election
    (PACE) 66
  proportional representation 8
  social justice through electoral politics
    5-14
poverty 19, 33, 110-11, 136-7, 140-1, 145
prisoners 88-108
  children with incarcerated parents 99
  citizenship, barriers to full 98
  class 92

coordination, lack of 103
costs of imprisonment 90
'country club' myth 91
employment for ex-prisoners 97, 98-9
family lives and relationships,
    disruption to 93-4, 99-100, 102
health, emotional and physical 94-5,
    103
housing for ex-prisoners 97, 98, 101
life in prison and impact on prisoners
    91, 93-6
minorities, disproportionate
    representation of 91-2, 99-100
pre-release programs 101-2
private industry 90
psychiatric treatment 92
punitive approach 89-91, 101-2
recidivism 96-7, 101
re-enfranchisement 6, 8-9
re-entry into community 90-1, 95-104
sentencing, public discourse on 88-90,
    101-2
statistics 88-91, 96-9
stigma 97
substance abuse 92-3, 97-8, 102-3
supervision of ex-prisoners 100
Supreme Court, rights of prisoners and
    70-2, 77
visits and telephone calls 93-4
who is imprisoned 91-3
women 92, 99, 102-3
problem-solving model of social policy 18-
    19, 21-3, 26
professional development 144
professional relationship building and
    networking 143, 145
proportional representation 8

race
    affirmative action 81-2, 84
    employment 72, 73-4, 77, 82-3
    school desegregation and affirmative
        action 81-2, 84
recidivism 96-7, 101
re-entry of prisoners into community 90-1,
    95-104
Rehnquist, William 68-70
reference tools 60
reproductive rights 70-1, 76-7, 81, 84

Roberts, John G 69, 70-1, 73-84

school desegregation and affirmative
    action 81-2, 84
sentencing, public discourse on 88-90,
    101-2
service learning 124-35
    AIDS awareness and prevention
        campaign 131
    community action programs 130
    community-based activities 132-3
    community needs assessments 128-9
    curriculum model 127-34
    field practice 125-6
    Human Behaviour in Organizations and
        Communities (HBOC) 127, 128-9,
        131
    Human Diversity and Social Justice
        (HDSJ) 127, 130-1
    implementation 132-3
    learning objectives to experiential-
        based experiences, linking 126
    macro-intervention 124-35
    research 129-30
    skill development 130, 133-4
    Social Welfare Policy 127, 129-31
    volunteering 132, 134
Settlement House Movement 52
Smart Mobs 67
skill development 130, 133-4
social action model 35-6
social bookmarking services 61
social capital
    advocacy 143
    bonding, bridging and linking 138-9,
        141-4
    community practice 140
    definition 137-8
    integration with education 142-4
    policy practice 141-2, 145-6
    poverty 136-7, 140-1, 145
    professional development 144
    professional relationship building and
        networking 143, 145
    social work education and practice
        136-48
    support networks 139, 140, 141
    welfare to work programs 146
social constructionist view of social policy

17-18, 22
social exclusion/inclusion 109-23
  agenda for research 119-20
  benefits of inclusion 115
  Centre for Social Development (CSD),
    Washington University 119-20
  conceptualizing 111-13
  cultural assimilation, inclusion as 120
  data inadequacies and collection 116-
    20
  disability, persons with a 112-13
  education and asset building 120
  elderly 113
  elimination of exclusion 109-10
  extent of exclusion 112-13
  functional areas 115-16
  human rights 113
  importance of inclusion 113-16
  measuring inclusion 116-18
  middle-range theory 119-20
  policy process, inclusion in 111, 114-21
  self-exclusion 120
  youth 113
social networking software 60-1
social or free software 50-1, 54-62
social planning policy model 35-6
social welfare
  reform 34-5
  service learning 127, 129-31
  Social Welfare Policy 127, 129-31
social work education *see also* service
  learning
  advocacy 66-7
  electronic advocacy 54-6, 62-3
  social capital 136-48
social work advocacy *see* advocacy
sexual orientation discrimination 76
spreadsheets 58-9
Stages of Change Model 46-8
strength-based framework for social policy
  barriers and possibilities 16-31
  blame, avoiding 22-3
  Chafee Act 24-5
  collaborative approach 29
  Educational and Training Voucher
    Programs (ETVPs) 25
  fear of change 28-9
  foster care, youths leaving 24-8
  key components 22-3

language 18, 22
long-term approach to change 29
National Association of Social Workers
  (NASW) 16-17
obstacles and opportunities 28-30
policy analysis and formation 20-4
practical feasibility 27-8
problem-solving model 18-19, 21-3, 26
relationships, placing premium on 27,
  29
social constructionist view 17-18, 22
success, definition of 29-30
symbols, icons and words, use of 17-18
time 28
value-based approach 20-4, 30
youth policy 24-8, 30
support networks 139, 140, 141
Supreme Court 68-87
  2005-2006 transitional term 73-7, 83-4
  2006-2007 opinions 78-84
  abortion 70-1, 76-7, 81, 84
  affirmative action 81-2, 84
  Alito, Samuel 69-70, 71-84
  assisted suicide, use of controlled drugs
    in 75
  capital punishment 77-8, 79
  church and state, separation of 72-3, 78
  civil rights in the Supreme Court 70-2,
    77-8, 81-2
  composition 68-70
  conservative and liberal positions
    68-70, 77-8, 84
  criminal defendants and prisoners,
    rights of 70-2, 77
  death penalty 77-8, 79
  deportation, immigration and 81
  disabled children, individual education
    programs (IEP) for 73, 83
  discrimination in employment 72, 73-4,
    77, 82-3
  duress 74
  election campaign expenditure and
    contributions 76
  freedom of speech 74-5, 76, 78, 79-80
  Guantanamo Bay, military
    commissions at 75-6
  immigration, deportation and 81
  National Association of Social Workers
    (NASW) 70-1

O'Connor, Sandra Day 68-70
Rehnquist, William 68-70
Roberts, John G 69, 70-1, 73-84
    school desegregation and affirmative
        action 81-2, 84
    sexual orientation discrimination 76
symbols, icons and words, use of 17-18

Tabblo 58
traditional social policy frameworks 18-20

value-based approach to social policy
    20-4, 30
volunteering 132, 134

wages 10 *see also* living wage movement,
    case study in

welfare reform 34-5
welfare to work programs 146
women
    discrimination in employment 72, 73-4,
        77, 82-3
    prison 92, 99, 102-3
    reproductive rights 70-1, 76-7,
        81, 84
word processing 58-9

youth *see also* education
    Chafee Act 24-5
    foster care, youths leaving 24-8
    social exclusion/inclusion 113
    strength-based framework for social
        policy 24-8, 30
YouTube 61

www.ingramcontent.com/pod-product-compliance
Ingram Content Group UK Ltd.
Pitfield, Milton Keynes, MK11 3LW, UK
UKHW020349010325
455677UK00021B/366